ENDORSEMENTS

"The *Family Office Navigator* is the breakthrough book of its domain. It's a must-read practical guide for families on their journey of setting up or redesigning their family office and an indispensable reference book for professionals in the domain."

Alexander Osterwalder, Co-founder of Strategyzer and award-winning author of *Business Model Generation*

"A timely and valuable source of guidance and insight, created through careful research and analysis, written in an accessible style. A must-read for families engaged in designing, perfecting and utilizing their family office to achieve their ambitions."

Alexander Scott, Chairman of Schroders Family Office Service, Director of FBN International and co-president of the Family Office Community of FBN and Trustee of Grosvenor Estate

"The family office journey is exciting and also full of pitfalls along the way. The *Family Office Navigator* and its fun, hands on activities provide practical tools any family can apply to their effort in setting up or re-vamping their family office."

Alexandre Van Damme, Chairman of Patrinvest

"The *Family Office Navigator* is not only a required reading for those thinking of or in the process of setting up a family office, but also those families who've already set one up. The *Navigator* gives a clear and detailed explanation of the best practices for any family offices looking to run their organisation with professionalism and success."

David Bain, Founder and Publisher of *Family Capital*

"There is too much advice on what to do to create an effective family office, but very little about how to make it happen. The *Navigator* is a new kind of reader—a "do-book" that leads a family through the actions they can take together to start, build, and continually redefine their family office. While most guides focus exclusively on financial elements, this one takes a more holistic view of total family wealth, including essential non-financial elements. It's an essential guide for every business family as they transition from their legacy business to a portfolio of family enterprises."

Dennis Jaffe, Advisor to enterprising families and author of *Wealth 3.0: The Future of Family Wealth Advising*

"The *Family Office Navigator* is a truly unique and engaging book by thought leaders in the family office field. It is a definite must read for all families who wish to establish a family office or wish to rethink their existing family office strategy. It provides practical, easy to use and insightful tools that can be immediately implemented in your family office activities."

Dino Tan, Senior Vice President & Head of Family Business Division, Singapore Economic Development Board

"At a time where families are faced with increased complexity and volatility, the *Family Office Navigator* is a must read for any family that wants to stay successful across generations. It will help you build and implement an effective family office strategy in an engaging and hands-on way."

Edouard Thijssen, CoFounder of Trusted Family

"The *Family Office Navigator* is a valuable toolkit for business-owning families at various stages of evolution. For families that are experienced and have a well-established family office, the *Navigator* can help them formulate a purpose, make key strategic decisions on how to deploy their investments to serve this purpose, and consider family governance education for sustained long-term success. For those with little or no experience with family offices, the *Navigator* is an equally valuable tool. It helps families set up a family office and begin a structured process to allocate individual or collective family wealth for investments, maintaining a thoughtful balance of assets that are either aligned with or diversified away from the legacy business."

Farhad Forbes, Co-Chairman of Forbes Marshall and Chairman of FBN International

"A practical and user-friendly tool for families and their advisors who wish to set up or redesign the family office. The *Navigator* guides and engages readers with step-by-step ideas and strategic processes – all in a playful way."

Judy Green, PhD. President of the Family Firm Institute

"The *Family Office Navigator* delves deeply into the nuances of sculpting a family office in line with the family's distinct needs and wishes. Despite our family office's century-long history, we are now turning to this book to guide the evolution of our family office for the coming generations."

Kazuto Fukuhara, Principal and Deputy CEO of the Fukuhara Group

"The *Family Office Navigator* is your quick-start, hands-on guide to inspire wealth creators, their advisors, and operators to shape their family office to reflect their needs. It is both educational and actionable, making it a perfect companion for any family looking for guidance during the setup of a new family office or during the process of transforming an existing one. Written for the layperson, this book is easy to read, full of visuals and helpful templates, and yet grapples with advanced family office topics. This will be a fantastic addition to your library."

Kirby Rosplock, PhD, CEO-Tamarind Partners and Tamarind Learning

"A highly valuable and very much needed tool to demystify different types of family offices and supporting families and their advisors to define the purpose, develop structures and implement governance that are customized to the needs of one family. This makes the *Family Office Navigator* so valuable and unique."

Peter Englisch, Partner, Global Family Business and EMEA Entrepreneurial & Private Business Leader bei PwC

"The *Family Office Navigator* provides valuable insights about how family offices support the broader family enterprise ecosystem, stating that 'it is paramount that families clearly define their overarching goals and aspirations as guidance for the family office.' This book provides a practical framework for the family to address critical questions in a logical order to shape the design of the family office and to select the most appropriate leaders to manage a professional office that evolves as the family evolves."

Sara Hamilton, Founder and Board Chair, Family Office Exchange

"An indispensable compass for families navigating the complex world of wealth management. The *Family Office Navigator* is your guide to shaping a lasting legacy, addressing both financial and non-financial aspects. A must-read for those committed to securing their family's future."

Susana Gallardo, President of the Board of the Gallardo Family Group and co-president of the Family Office Community of FBN

Peter Vogel
Mario Marconi

FAMILY OFFICE NAVIGATOR

Your Guide to Building a Multigenerational Family Office

IMD
Real learning
Real impact

Chemin de Bellerive 23
P.O. Box 915
CH – 1001 Lausanne
Switzerland
Tel: +41 21 618 01 11 – Fax: +41 21 618 07 07
www.imd.org

The right of Peter Vogel and Mario Marconi to be
identified as authors of this work has been asserted by
them in accordance with the Copyright, Designs and
Patents Act 1988.

Typeset in Basic Sans (Daniel Hernández, Latinotype),
Palomino (Elena Genova, My Creative Land)
and Pangolin (Kevin Bourke).

ISBN 978-2-940485-37-6
eISBN 978-2-940485-38-3

Designed by housatonic.eu

ACKNOWLEDGEMENTS

The crafting of the *Family Office Navigator* has been an enlightening voyage. Throughout this journey, we've had the honor of joining forces with numerous individuals, families, and organizations, to whom we express our deepest gratitude.

Our journey in crafting the *Family Office Navigator* was profoundly influenced by the invaluable learnings, stories, and feedback from remarkable individuals and families during interviews, workshops, webinars, and gatherings. Their insights, along with the narratives and lessons shared by families about their family office endeavors, have been instrumental in refining the content.

Special appreciation goes to our dedicated team members who have helped us bring this project to life, particularly Matt Falloon. With his unwavering enthusiasm, patience, and editorial prowess, he has been instrumental in this journey. Our heartfelt thanks to the design maestros from Housatonic: Alfredo Carlo, Veronica Maccari, Beatrice Schena, and Elena Vasumini. Their presence was felt not just in the book's production but throughout its entire conception, including the numerous workshops during its validation phase.

Furthermore, we're indebted to Courtney Collette, John Davis, Martin Liechti, and Marius Holzer from the Cambridge Family Enterprise Group for their valuable insights, countless feedback sessions, and overall contribution to the book, particularly in the face of the unexpected loss of our mutual friend and colleague, Mario.

A special thanks to Matthew Crudgington, Małgorzata Smulowitz, Anouk Lavoie, Nathalie Martin, and Virginie Boillat-Carrard from the IMD Global Family Business Center team. They have supported us in various ways throughout this journey, whether in brainstorming sessions, by reviewing frameworks and activities, assessing the designs, or cross-reading the final text.

We would also like to thank the wider IMD community, including IMD's president Jean-François Manzoni, for his generous support of our work in the Global Family Business Center and, more specifically, this project. Additionally, we acknowledge the tireless efforts of the editorial and communications teams.

A warm acknowledgment goes to the Family Business Network, especially Alexis Du Roy de Blicquy, Farhad Forbes, Christine Gaucher, Alexander Scott, Susana Gallardo, and the entire FBN Board. Their unwavering support and assistance in connecting us with families globally for interviews enriched our understanding of family office dynamics.

This work stands testament to the wisdom of countless individuals and organizations with whom we've collaborated over the years. The *Family Office Navigator* embodies a collective spirit, underlining the significance of a cohesive ecosystem for a triumphant family office journey. We fervently advocate for collaboration, exchange, and shared growth. Here's to your inspiring journey ahead!

With gratitude,

Peter Vogel, on behalf of the authors

Alfredo Beatrice
Veronica Elena

Alexis
Farhad
Christine
Susana
Alexander

Matt

THANK YOU !

Jean-François

Courtney
John Martin
Marius

Anouk Matthew
Małgorzata Virginie
Nathalie

MEET THE TEAM

PETER VOGEL

"To my co-author and friend, Mario, who left us far too early."

In my role as Professor and Director of the IMD Global Family Business Center, I have the privilege of working with enterprising families from around the world. My ultimate goal is to assist them in ensuring multi-generational success and unity. Many of these families either have a family office or are in the midst of establishing one. My mission is to guide them through the intricate terrains of a family office in the most effective and efficient manner.

This has motivated me to create the *Family Office Navigator*, the second in a series of *Navigator* books, following the publication of the *Family Philanthropy Navigator* in 2020.

I hope this book will challenge, educate, and inspire families in their family office endeavors, irrespective of whether they are novices in the realm of family offices or have accrued decades of experience. In the end, I envision the *Navigator* evolving into a standalone tool that families and their advisors worldwide will find invaluable.

MARIO MARCONI

"To life, to the future."

Mario was passionate about his work and always recognized the wider purpose and values in each entrepreneurial family. He had the privilege of meeting and assisting numerous families around the world, especially on topics where they could make a difference in people's lives. His deep desire was to transmit knowledge to meet the family's needs and empower younger generations. He was honored to co-write the *Family Office Navigator* with Peter Vogel, sharing their collective wisdom.

Unfortunately, Mario left us too early to complete this project about which he cared so deeply. Our gratitude extends to Peter as well as Mario's colleagues at CFEG who supported its realization. This book will not only be valued for its written words, but its completion is also proof that the union of families and friendships can lead to the accomplishment of wonderful projects.

In memory of Mario, we hope this book will stand as one of the pillar stones that protect and bind families together, not only in good times but also in challenging ones.

Ivana, Filippo, and Leonardo Marconi (Mario's Family)

MATT FALLOON

As the lead editor for the *Family Office Navigator*, it was a great personal and professional privilege for me to work with Peter, Mario, and the rest of the team in bringing their exceptional levels of knowledge, skill, expertise, and experience together in a meaningful and impactful way for our audience.

With this book, we have strived to create and present a practical, easy-to-understand – but also deeply comprehensive – guide and framework that we hope will help families shape healthy and positive futures for the generations to come, and for society at large.

COURTNEY COLLETTE, MARTIN LIECHTI, MARIUS HOLZER

"To all enterprising families, on their multigenerational journeys, in this turbulent world."

At Cambridge Family Enterprise Group, serving enterprising families is what motivates us. We continually strive to better understand and respond to the ever-changing challenges and opportunities that families and their enterprises face. Our services have evolved over the years, and – with the visionary leadership of Mario Marconi – have deepened, to support family offices as a vehicle for family success and wealth regeneration.

Developing the *Family Office Navigator* with Peter had been a passion for Mario these past few years. Though he was unable to see the fruits of their efforts in the publication of this book, we were sad but proud to step up to the task of completing the book in Mario's honor, in collaboration with Peter. It is our hope that it will be a testimonial to Mario, as well as an invaluable tool for enterprising families as they build and strengthen their family offices for generations to come.

ALFREDO CARLO, VERONICA MACCARI, BEATRICE SCHENA AND ELENA VASUMINI

"To Mario, it's been great and too short knowing you."

Our design studio, Housatonic, exists to create bridges toward generative relationships, where design plays a key role. We worked on the design of this book with the hope that anyone will be able to use it to enhance the way we create a positive impact on the planet. We believe that good design promotes good collaboration, and that collaboration is the only factor that will allow us to make the changes needed to create a better future for all, including our own families.

We hope the *Family Office Navigator* book will not only help readers better understand how to shape each family's vision and future but also focus on what's relevant with intention and sound organization.

FOREWORD

by John Davis

> The Family Office Navigator offers enterprising families a comprehensive and practical guide to design a modern family office that considers the complexity of their family, wealth, and enterprise in turbulent times.

We are living in an unprecedented time in history. The events unfolding in the world around us are dramatically impacting owning families and their enterprises. Ever-shifting global forces - including ecological, technological, geopolitical, economic, and societal changes - create relentless turbulence, significant challenges, occasional disruption, and some exciting opportunities for enterprising families. The same can be said about the changes happening inside families, inside businesses, and inside family offices. It is crucial to understand how our changing world is impacting family enterprises and enterprising families, and to identify what they can, and must, do to be future-ready.

Many enterprising families today are learning about Family Offices, and some are launching them—sometimes these launches are premature. We should learn about these flexible and useful organizations. Peter Vogel and Mario Marconi describe the history and evolution of family offices, explaining their surge in importance and numbers in recent years. The growth in interest in this relatively new vehicle for family investments and family support is due to the mountain of liquid wealth generated mostly by operating businesses over the last decades and a desire by enterprising families to have greater control over the direction of their wealth. But family offices can help enterprising families in so many ways.

From my vantage point, enterprising families are in a period of learning about and testing this new model. A properly designed and run family office can have many benefits for a family. In addition to overseeing the management of its wealth, advising the family on legal and financial matters, and supporting the diverse activities of a family, a family office can help the family learn about its environment and new trends, and ultimately grow the family's resources, talent, and unity so it can survive and be adaptive. Peter and Mario will help you understand these benefits and how to achieve them.

After all, families have much to do to maintain their success in this era. Families aspiring to multigenerational success have a three-pronged agenda: grow and transfer their wealth, keep family members united, and develop family members to contribute to their enterprise. These are complex tasks, and having a family office to focus on them and execute the family's multigenerational strategy is a great resource. In turbulent times such as the one we are in these tasks require new mindsets and approaches. Family offices can help you develop these. In fact, some of the most innovative solutions that I am seeing in family enterprises today are stimulated by family offices. It is essential for families to develop agile and innovative family offices for the future.

Consider investment management – the original raison d'être of a family office for many owners. Investment vehicles are constantly being reinvented. Economic and other uncertainties abound. Technological innovations are transforming asset management. Family offices must keep up with these changes.

What does the family office of the future look like? The *Family Office Navigator* delves into the many available choices and adaptations. Peter and Mario do not present a "one size fits all" model, but rather a set of options to be customized and continually evolved to meet the needs of families and enterprises.

As families and their enterprises grow and become increasingly complex and diverse, families are broadening their view of the family office. The family office of the future looks more like an ambidextrous corporate office for the family and owners, playing a strategic and integrative role for families and their entire collection of shared assets and activities. It is an important bridge between the family and its holdings, and among family members themselves. Family office activities going forward could include a family's total wealth strategy, its social impact activities including family philanthropy, family governance, family unity, family talent development, and family succession, plus a variety of technological, personal, and administrative services.

As its name implies, this book is designed to help wealth owners navigate the family office terrain, whether building one from scratch or improving an existing organization. It helps owners to structure important conversations and gain consensus among family members about their family office, in the context of what they want to accomplish and their values as a family.

The *Family Office Navigator* closes with a call to action, challenging owners to take a learning mindset and think of this as a family office journey. This resonates with my deep conviction that owners need to be agile to survive in today's fast-paced business world. You must be willing and able to continually scan for and adapt to changes impacting your family enterprise, including your family office.

This book is just the latest collaboration between IMD and CFEG. I am proud of our long relationship. I co-founded IMD's family business program in 1988 and was delighted when Peter took it over in 2019. He has innovated and grown IMD's programs to serve as a meaningful resource for family enterprises. Mario, my esteemed CFEG colleague and dear friend, sadly passed away during the writing of this book. He and Peter now provide us with an essential guide and toolkit on the timely and crucial topic of the family office.

As you become ready to build your family office of the future and navigate these turbulent times with an expert guide, the *Family Office Navigator* is here to help.

PROFESSOR JOHN A. DAVIS

Chairman and Founder, Cambridge Family Enterprise Group
Senior Lecturer and Faculty Director, Family Enterprise,
MIT Sloan School of Management

CHAPTER 1

GET READY FOR YOUR FAMILY OFFICE JOURNEY

Let's embark on the journey towards building a new family office or repurposing an existing one.

Welcome to the *Family Office Navigator*. This practical guidebook and easy-to-use tool is designed to inspire and empower families to navigate and enjoy the rewarding journey towards building a new family office or repurposing an existing one.

THE PURPOSE OF THE FAMILY OFFICE NAVIGATOR

Over the past decades we have been fortunate to work with hundreds of enterprising families from around the world – both as academics and trusted advisors – and support them in their family office journeys.

Through our work, it has become clear that families face similar challenges when it comes to establishing or redesigning a family office. Central to these challenges is a shortage of information about what family offices are and how they work, how they evolve, and how they last across generations, as well as where to turn for sensible advice and what to do at critical junctures.

Our goal with this book is to empower families to successfully navigate the complex world of family offices by equipping them with the knowledge and tools to take informed decisions as they build a high-performing family office. The result is the *Family Office Navigator*.

The *Family Office Navigator* will assist you in creating a roadmap to establish and run a professional family office–one that serves as a holistic platform that preserves your family enterprise ecosystem and manages your family's total wealth and other affairs. The book will help you answer critical questions and take important decisions while equipping you with practical frameworks and recommended actions for your family office journey. It will give you the necessary tools to talk with your family and to engage with outside experts as you manage the process.

It is important to us that all members of a family, regardless of their financial acumen, are informed about family offices so they can be capable wealth owners and supportive clients of their family office. What you will find in these pages is grounded in rigorous thought leadership and extensive practice, but presented in a conversational manner so everyone in your family - not just those leading business and financial matters - can understand and make use of the book.

The *Family Office Navigator* will help you:

- **Demystify the family office (Chapter 1)** and the role it can play in a family enterprise ecosystem, and understand the trends shaping this function

- **Chart your course (Chapter 2)**, so that you can assess why you are considering this journey, what you currently have as a family, and where you want to go in the future

- **Define the purpose (Chapter 3)** of your family office, including your motivation, aspiration and goals, covering both financial and non-financial objectives

- **Decide on the focus (Chapter 4)** of your family office by identifying the activities your family office needs to support at this time

- **Organize your family office (Chapter 5)** for effective management of resources, efficient structures, sensible monitoring and good governance

- **Embed a learning mindset (Chapter 6)** into your family office journey to continually improve your family office's performance over time

Why is there increased interest in family offices globally?

	Increasing numbers	• Overall increase in wealth (HNWI / UHNWI) worldwide • Rise of a new class of mega wealth owners due to digital revolution • Rise of wealthy families in Asia
	Increasing complexity of family, ownership & business (FOB)	• Cross-border assets and families • Exposure to different national and international regulations and systems (admin, tax, legal, etc.), demanding close monitoring and professional, customized management
	Increasing complexity of investments	• The world around us is becoming increasingly complex • Families with to gain exposure to new / different investment opportunities, traditionally not served by banks (e.g., crypto, SPACs)
	Trendiness / glamour of having a family office	• There's a hype around family offices • Many think that setting up a family office is the ultimate goal

Over the past decades we have witnessed a massive increase in the number of family offices around the world. Consequently, the family office industry, including a vast array of services, has evolved. One can now find plenty of resources, including academic studies and courses, conferences for various stakeholders in the space, practitioners who specialize in advising family offices on multiple dimensions, emerging technologies, infrastructure to increase efficiencies within family offices, specialized services for family offices provided by financial institutions, and an increasing body of knowledge about family office performance.

The increased spotlight has been in response to the growing interest by families for guidance, expertise, data, talent, and best practices for how to set up or strengthen their own family office.

This recent momentum has been fuelled by several trends, including:

- The massive transfer of wealth to a new generation that is taking the reins of family businesses
- The rise of a new category of wealth owners who have made their fortune in the digital revolution
- The growth in the number of wealthy families in Asia
- Families' desire to hedge against global instability by diversifying assets beyond their legacy operating company
- A desire by families to have greater control and transparency regarding how their assets are invested
- A desire for greater privacy for families
- A certain trendiness, glamour, and social status associated with owning a family office

---

At the same time, the demand for more professionalized family offices has grown as an increasing number of family office organizations mature and aspire to higher professional standards, elevating the global benchmark for high-functioning family offices.

Meanwhile, the level of complexity in family enterprises and families is rising, which is also leading more families to explore the option of setting up a family office. The range of activities families engage in – as owners, business leaders, investors, and community leaders–has become increasingly complex. Look at the world of investments, which has become more complicated and fast-paced, resulting in a wide range of investment opportunities that are not always easy to understand and navigate. More recent examples that have drawn the attention of both individual investors and family offices include cryptocurrencies and SPACS (special purpose acquisition company). These resulted in attractive, and rather sudden, returns for some investors, while leaving others with significant losses.

Not only is the world of business and investments diverse and complex today, but families are, too. They are more geographically dispersed than in prior generations which requires them to have to grapple with an intricate web of national and international legal, tax, inheritance, and citizenship systems and regulations. This geographic dispersion is accompanied by more individual-centric lives, careers, interests, and needs on the part of family members. That means the wealth management of their common assets needs customization, and families need to work harder to remain unified and connected, both emotionally and financially.

Because of this increased complexity, families are turning to family offices as vehicles to serve their specialized needs through bespoke services. A family office can act as a unifying, central, organizing vehicle that provides a family with an aggregate view of all their businesses, investments, donations, assets, and other activities. The more integrated the family office is with the family's larger family enterprise ecosystem, the more it can support the vision, strategy, and needs of the broader system, rather than operating as a silo. For example, families are increasingly leaning on family offices to help plan proactively for generational succession to enhance the sustainability and success of the businesses, investments, and bloodlines over time. A family office is considered by many to be the logical next step for a family in business.

As overall distrust in institutions rises, partially fuelled by scandals in the investment world, it is more important than ever for families to sit in the driving seat when managing their investments and steering their family enterprise. If organized well, a family office can be the right place for a family to exercise their active participation, ownership, direction, and oversight.

Why a Family Office Navigator?

We've established that there is an unprecedented demand for family offices as a platform to support families and, in response, a rapid increase in the number of family offices around the world seeking guidance, especially in the beginning of the journey. No family office can operate without external resources and partners, so at the same time, the number of service firms in this domain has skyrocketed. The result for families is a large, unwieldly sandbox, making it challenging to navigate this space, know what support they might need and who the right partner might be. It is therefore of critical importance that families feel empowered and in charge of their family office journey – knowing exactly what they are looking for, what types of questions to ask, how to assess the answers they receive, and how to execute the right plan for their situation. This allows a family to set off confidently and successfully from the get-go.

Setting up or repurposing a family office is, typically, a once-in-a-generation event (though any long-lasting organization reinvents itself as often as conditions call for it). The creation of a family office is often triggered by a capital inflow, whether from a liquidity event which pushes the family to organize its assets so they do not lose out on financial opportunities, or a profitable operating company paying out dividends that the owners want to deploy into other investments. Regardless of the triggering event, going through this initial design phase in haste, without proper internal reflection and alignment about the purpose and focus of the family office, and without the right outside partners, can prove costly.

It is the responsibility of the family owners to select competent advisors who put the family's interests at the heart of their endeavors, and who instil in the family and family office the capabilities they need to become self-sustaining when the time is right. The *Family Office Navigator* starts by guiding families through this initial reflection and design phase of their family office journey.

Let's face it, fulfilling many of the responsibilities of family offices requires specialized knowledge that is challenging to gain without direct experience. For this reason, families must have capable specialists overseeing, for example, their asset allocation, compliance with financial regulations, the quality of their legal agreements, and the functioning of their family governance. Assembling the right team of internal and external experts is paramount. Advisors can be extremely useful to help families navigate liquidity events, set up family offices or formalize services that have, until now, been handled by family members. However, it can be tempting to parcel out this work completely, delegating it to external advisors (to a private banker, attorney or family governance advisor, for instance). Yet no family should delegate this work to a provider without having a point of view or without being able to provide high-level goals, and even direction, to guide the outcomes.

We know that taking a passive role and relying too heavily on outsiders, without giving them the necessary guidance and direction from the family, can lead to sub-optimal outcomes and a lack of cohesion across your family enterprise ecosystem. Far too many family offices and external advisors do not add the value they could to the family they are serving, in part because the family does not provide a sufficiently clear owners' vision and strategy. It is paramount that families clearly define their overarching goals and aspirations as guidance for the family office. Through the *Family Office Navigator*, we want to empower you and your family, and provide you with the necessary knowledge and tools to lead the stakeholders on your family office journey.

While there is an abundance of literature designed for professionals, there is limited material that has been specifically designed for enterprising families, that is both accessible and practical in nature. We therefore aim to bridge the knowledge gap as more and more families look to create or strengthen their own family offices. The *Family Office Navigator* builds on decades of experience working with and teaching families from across the globe, combined with our global study on the purpose and evolution of family offices. With this knowledge base, we demystify the world of family offices and break it down into simple steps so that anyone in your family can understand and contribute to it.

Whether a family is early in its exploration of creating a family office or is experienced at running one, the *Family Office Navigator* provides guidance for all stages of the family office life cycle. The initial phase is of critical importance as it marks the beginning of a new era as you and your family enter unknown territories; it is therefore key that you and your family take sufficient time to reflect on some key questions surrounding the purpose and overarching aspirational goals to lay the foundation for your future family office. Families that already have a family office, whether formal or informal, also need to regularly think about whether it is still set up in the most effective and efficient way to meet their family's changing needs. Tools for every stage are found within this guidebook.

We are glad that you are here to empower yourself – in whatever stage your family office lies.

An ecosystem perspective – keeping your house in order

Before going further, it is important to offer key definitions and conceptual frameworks that we will refer to throughout the book, namely:

- **Family enterprise ecosystem**
- **The health of your family enterprise ecosystem**
- **Total family wealth**

These frameworks and concepts are inter-related. They look at the big picture of what you are trying to build in your family office endeavors from different perspectives. Throughout the book, we will use these frameworks and recommend that you apply them in your family discussions as well.

Family Enterprise Ecosystem

Imagine your family as an environmental ecosystem, such as a coral reef. We use this visual metaphor because we see some parallels between family enterprise ecosystems with the natural world and strongly believe in the power of metaphors to help everyone in the family imagine their own ecosystem. A coral reef is a diverse underwater ecosystem made up of colonies of tiny living organisms which, along with other organisms (like algae, sponges, and fish), create a complex and colourful environment that provides food, shelter, and protection for a wide variety of marine life. The health of this reef depends on countless factors, some environmental, some internal, some familiar, some unanticipated.

Building on this visual metaphor, your family enterprise ecosystem contains all the actors and factors that comprise your family and its network - your core family and wider family circles, your business(es) and investments, your assets, your philanthropic activities, your homes, your relationships within the family and beyond, your service providers and employees. Outside of your family and its various assets and resources are all of the external elements and actors that influence your enterprise ecosystem - the economic and political environment you are embedded in, including regulations, market dynamics and competitors, political systems, tax authorities, banks and your immediate community, for example.

For the purpose of this book, we define a Family Enterprise Ecosystem as follows:

"A Family Enterprise Ecosystem is a dynamic and evolving system that includes all aspects related to your family, the businesses and other assets that your family owns, the way in which you govern the family, ownership, businesses & wealth, as well as your role in society and impact on the environment."

While we will delve deeper into this in the "Charting your Course" chapter, we would like to provide you with an introduction to this concept here in order to illustrate how complex and "rich" your own family enterprise ecosystem actually is. Your family office will serve many dimensions of your ecosystem, so it is vital that you map out all its elements and define where the family office will fit within the broader ecosystem.

It is important to note that no two ecosystems are identical. While some core dimensions might be similar, your ecosystem is distinctly different from any other family's ecosystem.

The key dimensions of your family enterprise ecosystem are expressed through the following questions:

Who are we as a family?

What do we own?

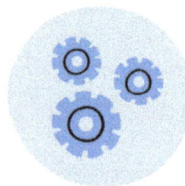

How are we organized?

What is our role in society, and our impact on the environment?

We will come back to these dimensions later in the book as they form the basis of many of the activities that we have put together for you and your family.

The Health of your Family Enterprise Ecosystem

As in any ecosystem, the overall health of the system and its inhabitants is of critical importance for long-term survival. All factors and actors are inter-dependent.

It is our belief that any family enterprise ecosystem can only be successful in the long run if the family carefully manages five areas:

1. The individuals in the ecosystem
2. The family
3. Ownership
4. Businesses activities
5. Broader society and the environment

We illustrate the five dimensions that collectively represent a healthy family enterprise ecosystem in the Five Stone Model.

Society & environment — Family enterprises as a force for good through their sustainability efforts, impact investing, philanthropy and striving toward making a positive collective impact.

Business — Effective leadership and governance of businesses within the ecosystem with a solid long-term oriented growth strategy and healthy financials.

Ownership — Capable, well-educated and emotionally connected owners with solid ownership governance.

Family — Strong family relations with unity and trust, as well as solid family governance.

Individuals — Educated, capable and interested individuals with good physical and mental health as a basis for being effective contributors to the system.

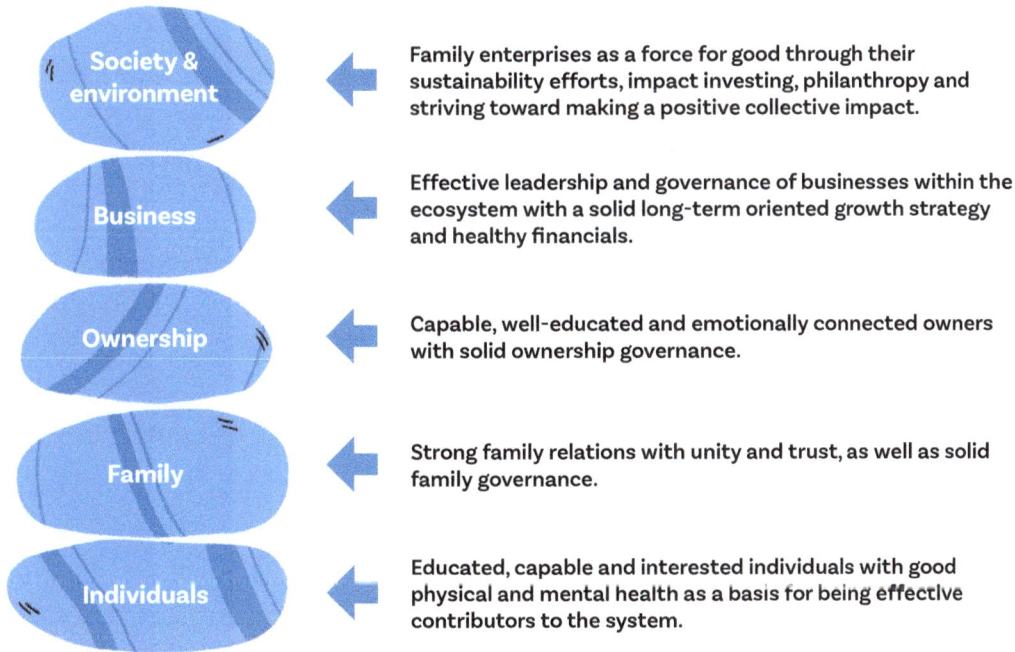

The family office can be the glue and catalyst for an enterprising family to keep its house in order, to support all these dimensions, and to reduce the risk of any cracks or imbalances in the ecosystem that might threaten its viability. If your family office is effective, it can help you and your family maintain a healthy family ecosystem. If it is ineffective, parts of the ecosystem might struggle to function or survive – perhaps even the whole ecosystem will suffer.

For instance, the family office can help to arrange education for family members or offer access to services to improve physical and mental wellbeing – this is the bottom stone, representing **Individuals**. The family office can provide lifestyle or concierge services. It can support the building of trust, good governance, and unity within a family – this is the **Family** stone. The family office can also empower and develop current and future business owners to ensure effective future leadership and healthy companies. It can help owners establish and practice good governance. It can improve the way the businesses and investment activities operate and the way the family supports its growth. It can also act as the nexus between the owners and the businesses and investments in case the family is no longer operationally active. These functions correspond to the **Ownership** stone or the **Business** dimension. Lastly, the family office can help optimize the impact of the family on society and the environment and foster a cohesive strategy across the family's full activities – from business to investments to philanthropy – illustrated in the **Society & Environment** stone at the top of the structure.

In the "Charting your Course" chapter, you will have a chance to engage in a high-level discussion with your family. You will map out your own family enterprise ecosystem, assess its overall health and gain clarity on the various complexities that might exist within your ecosystem. This will serve as the basis to explore possible family office services, which we will examine further in the "Focus" chapter.

Total Family Wealth

The richness and beauty of the coral reef comes from the diversity of organisms and species that make up the ecosystem. Similarly, families are worth much more than their financial assets, and the most enduring and successful families understand the importance of preserving and nurturing all the elements in their family enterprise ecosystem.

Therefore, within this ecosystem, we refer to the primary scope and mandate of the family office as preserving and managing "total family wealth," not just financial wealth. We often speak of the family's treasure chest.

For the purpose of this book, we define total family wealth as follows:

"Total Family Wealth encompasses human, social, financial, reputational, intellectual, and other forms of capital, representing the overall wealth of a family enterprise ecosystem beyond its financial means."

Human capital
Human capital refers to the knowledge, skills, experiences, and abilities of all the individuals within the family that can contribute to the overall success and prosperity of the family. This can include education, professional training, work experience, relationships, and personal qualities. One might also consider it to include the physical and psychological well-being of individual family members.

Financial capital
Financial capital refers to the family's financial assets, including cash, investments, physical assets such as real estate, artwork or collectable items, and other resources that can be used to generate income, build wealth and support the family's needs and goals. Financial capital can be used for a variety of purposes, including investments and other business-related matters, covering family expenses and engaging in philanthropic endeavours. Building and managing financial capital is an important part of ensuring the long-term stability and prosperity of a family.

Intellectual capital
Intellectual capital refers to the family's intangible assets, such as patents, trademarks, copyrights, and other proprietary knowledge and information. By investing in and managing its intellectual capital, a family can build a sustainable competitive advantage, generate income and build new sources of wealth.

Social capital
Social capital refers to the networks, relationships, and connections within the family and with external organizations and individuals that can help the family achieve its goals. Strong bonds, unity and trust are of essence for the long-term success of a family enterprise ecosystem. Strong external relationships, such as networks of friends, business contacts, community connections, and other relationships that provide the family with access to information, resources and support can provide a family with a competitive advantage, help it to overcome challenges and thrive.

Reputational capital
The reputational capital of a family refers to the collective reputation and image that a family has built over time, which can positively or negatively affect their standing in society, their business dealings, and personal relationships. This reputation is influenced by factors such as the family's actions, behavior, relationships, accomplishments, and cultural or social contributions. A positive reputation can open doors and create opportunities, while a negative one can limit them.

The combination of these different types of capital can contribute to the overall wealth and success of a family.

For many families, of course, the family office is primarily a vehicle to manage financial capital (for example, after a liquidity event). However, we believe that family offices function best – and deliver the greatest positive impact to the long-term health of the family enterprise ecosystem – when all forms of family wealth are considered and addressed in planning and decision-making.

Looking at family financial returns alone, without considering the bigger picture, such as the family's overall purpose, its needs and wants and the legal or tax implications of a given strategy on a multi-generational timescale, might lead to unwanted surprises and an unhealthy ecosystem. Focusing exclusively on building wealth while ignoring the importance of developing human and social capital for the future can lead to wealth destruction in the next generation, perhaps because of growing conflicts and tensions, or inadequate family talent to set direction and oversee activities, or a lack of a collective value creation mindset.

In contrast, looking at all aspects of your family's wealth as an inter-connected system is the best approach to ensure multi-generational success and unity. This holistic mindset will ultimately help you design the most effective and efficient family office that delivers on your goals.

A family office can be whatever you want it to be, and it can play different roles at different stages. Within a cohesive family enterprise ecosystem, where families seek to align all their activities as part of their common goals, the family office plays a vital, coordinating role. It can be the platform that houses, supports and connects all the different activities and interests within the family ecosystem.

As we move through the *Family Office Navigator*, we encourage you to think of the family office as a custodian tasked with managing your Total Family Wealth and ensuring that your constantly evolving Family Enterprise Ecosystem is in good health.

Why families consider setting up a family office

There are many reasons why families think about setting up a new family office or repurposing an existing one. For some, a family office becomes an obvious next step after a liquidity event such as the sale of a business. For others, a family office is created out of the desire for more control or independence from financial institutions or to achieve better investment outcomes. Beyond these initial triggers, there are many other motivations for having a family office, such as to protect family privacy, to foster family unity, to develop family talent, to support intra-family ownership and leadership succession, to offer tailored services to the family or to support family and ownership governance. For a few, it's a status-driven pursuit. For others, it's a vehicle for multigenerational wealth preservation. For many, it's a combination of different reasons.

Next, we will present the primary reasons why families establish a family office based on our research and work with enterprising families. As you read through them, we recommend that you and your family spend time together and reflect on which apply to you. Why are you interested in a family office for your family? Why is your family interested in creating one? Have an open and honest conversation with your family members because these reasons can vary from person to person.

This exploration is the first step toward ultimately defining the purpose of your family office, so it is important not to skip this activity. Make a note of the ones that apply to you and your family members because we will return to the significance of these factors in the next chapters.

Manage greater liquidity

The most common reason for families to consider setting up a family office is that they have a liquidity event from selling (part of or all of) a business, or they receive significant liquidity from the dividends of a profitable business they hold shares in. Greater liquidity creates a large amount of capital within the family that they wish to invest together and that needs to be managed.

Preserve family wealth

The family wishes to protect and sustain the value of its wealth in the present and the future to ensure the prosperity of the next generations.

Achieve excellence in investment management

The family feels it is not getting the returns or quality of service it wants from their existing investment management options and seeks higher levels of service and superior solutions.

Desire to delegate the burden of wealth management

The family requires expert help to improve the way it invests its wealth and to reduce the stress and time associated with financial management.

Wish for personalization and customization

The family has specific needs that require thoughtful solutions that are not catered to in a satisfactory way by its current setup or partners.

Next generation repurposing their family's assets

The next generation inherits the family's assets and wishes to reorganize or restructure the investments, their management, or their oversight according to their generation's preferences.

Active deal sourcing and pipeline management

The family wants to diversify its investments to explore emerging areas such as impact investment, venture capital, or direct investment.

Desire for more control, more independence, and more attention

The family wants greater autonomy and agility in setting, changing, and overseeing their investment strategy. They also prefer dedicated in-house management to be wholly focused on their assets and their affairs.

Support family and ownership governance

The family seeks support to better govern the family enterprise. First-rate family-, ownership- and investment governance are key to achieving long-term objectives because they provide direction and oversight and they promote strategic decision-making.

Protect family privacy, anonymity and confidentiality

The family wants to bring some or all of its affairs into a secure space that safeguards the family and reduces interference from the outside.

Consolidated reporting and centralized risk management

The family wants to improve oversight and risk management by creating a dedicated, centralized capability for all its affairs and activities.

Create a hub for the family

The family wants to build a central point of focus that fosters unity and cohesion across its various branches, including elements such as family bonding and talent development.

Separate family matters from business matters

Often, in the early stages of the life of an entrepreneur, the private matters of the family are taken care of by the company (e.g., legal, tax, investments are managed by company executives). Over time, families want to (or have to) create a formal separation between their private matters and the business.

Status

The family wants to set up a family office as a symbol of status and success, or for other reasons that do not have a specific or fundamental basis in supporting the family enterprise ecosystem.

As you explore the options and questions that arise from these triggering events or transitional moments, many questions may be crossing your mind. How do you know whether a family office is right for your family and future generations? How do you design a family office to ensure the health of your family's ecosystem? Is your individual and collective wealth being managed in the best way possible? Will your family office help you achieve your goals? Is your family office working as efficiently and effectively as it could? Do you have the right outside advisors to complement and partner with your family and with non-family leadership? Do you have the talent needed to professionally plan and execute your investment strategy in-house? Is your family skilled at overseeing a family office organization? Do you even need a family office in the first place?

We will return to these questions in the "Purpose" chapter later in the book.

DEMYSTIFYING THE FAMILY OFFICE

In recent decades, the family office has gained momentum as a must-have vehicle for successful entrepreneurs and enterprising families. There is a lot of buzz – and, let's face it, confusion – around the role of family offices. What are they really intended to do?

Family offices come in all shapes and sizes: When you have seen one family office, you have seen one family office. When it comes to the question of whether or not a family office is the right structure for you and your family, or whether or not your existing family office is still aligned with your family's overall purpose, it helps to start with some big questions. What is your and your family's current situation? How did you get here? What are you trying to achieve? Will a family office help you get there? Do you know enough about what a family office can do to answer these questions?

For the purpose of this book, we define a family office as follows:

"A Family Office is a more or less formal and constantly evolving organization or private office dedicated to one or more wealthy families with the mandate of managing their human, social and financial capital, as well as other affairs in the family enterprise ecosystem, with the objective of continuing the family heritage for the generations to come."

Most family offices cater to a myriad of needs for families to ensure that their houses are in order and that all aspects of their family enterprise ecosystems operate at their best. The most common services a family office provides are: investment and asset management, advisory on various matters related to the family, ownership, business and wealth, legal, tax, estate planning, accounting, education, real estate management, concierge services, governance support, philanthropic activities, administration, succession planning, and other personal services.

No matter why or how the family office comes into existence, think of it as more than just a means to manage financial wealth. It can become a powerful platform to support the overall health and well-being of the whole family enterprise ecosystem.

The type of family office or family office services that you and your family might consider is highly dependent on your personal and professional context. Family offices look very different depending on your overall level of wealth, family size and complexity, asset complexity, geographical hub, and desire or need for personalized services, among many other factors.

Later in the book, we will dive deeper into each of these areas so that you can take qualified decisions about the family office services that are important for you, keeping in mind that most family offices rarely start out with the full spectrum of capabilities. They evolve over time, adjusting to the changing needs of the family.

The history of the family office

We believe it is helpful for you to have a historical perspective of the family office, and how it has changed over time. Understanding why these changes have taken place allows us to appreciate the role that family offices play now and will play in the future as your context continues to change.

The family office – or some form of it – has been in existence for as long as there have been wealthy and powerful families. Today, we are in what we call the fourth wave of the family office, where the model has evolved to meet the needs of enterprising families in a highly uncertain, complex and rapidly changing world.

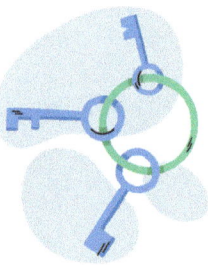

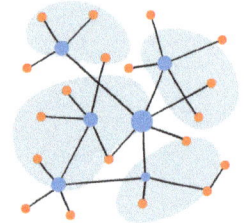

1st WAVE	2nd WAVE	3rd WAVE	4th WAVE
Major Domus / Majordomo	**Emergence of Trusts**	**First Formal Family Offices**	**Modern Family Offices**
In ancient Rome, this was "the highest person of a household staff, a head servant who acts on behalf of the owner of a large or significant residence."	Developed as an important tool for inter-generational wealth transfer in the UK in the 12th century during the time of the crusades.	Industrialists generated significant wealth during the industrial revolution and needed new ways to manage their wealth and businesses – e.g., House of Morgan (1838) / Rockefeller family office (1882).	Emergence of MFOs (e.g., Rockefeller Capital Management), the digital revolution, globalization, the rise of Asia and many other trends lead to a professionalization and diversification of the FO sector.

The first wave

In ancient Rome, influential families employed a senior staff member to manage the family's affairs. The "major domus" – supervisor of the household – was the highest ranked servant and acted on behalf of the owner of the residence, taking charge of the administration of the estate. This is one of first traces of a formalized governance and administrative role in the context of affluent families with the actual mandate to "keep the family's house in order." It wasn't called a family office at that time, but some of the core principles of modern family offices can be traced back to those early days.

The second wave

When English noblemen joined the Crusades during the Middle Ages, they left behind estates and family wealth for unpredictable periods of time. To manage these responsibilities in accordance with the wishes of the absent head of the household, trusts were developed as an important tool for inter-generational wealth transfer. This led to a split between the roles of the legal owner and the beneficial owner, with the legal owner being the "trustee" and the beneficial owner being the "beneficiary." Modern versions of these original trust structures are used frequently around the globe today.

The third wave

The first formal family offices emerged in the 19th century during the Industrial Revolution as newly wealthy entrepreneurial families such as the Rockefellers and Morgans sought effective ways to manage their wealth and business empires. This led to the creation of structured offices, such as the House of Morgan in 1838 and the Rockefeller Family Office in 1882. Some of these family offices still exist today and have evolved into financial powerhouses – both for the founding family and other unrelated families.

The fourth wave

The fourth wave gave rise to a number of variations in the family office model. For over a century, the original formal offices remained in place, following the same principles of setup and governance: one family with a private family office to cater to its needs. In the second half of the 20th century, some of these "single family" offices opened their doors to other unrelated families and became "multi family" offices, in part to defray the costs associated with increasingly sophisticated financial services.

Since then, the concept of a family office has evolved further. The first decades of the 21st century have led to the evolution of a wide array of vehicles that cater to the varied needs of modern-day family enterprise ecosystems. Modern family offices are more professional and specialized organizations that have been shaped by the digital revolution, globalization, and the rise of the Asian economy, among other trends. In fact, we refer to the "uberization" of the family office, with the emergence of hybrid family offices, sometimes also called "virtual family offices" or "family-office-as-a-service." The hybrid approach serves the holistic needs of the family by a network of providers, possibly combining in-house and external services.

Family office archetypes

There is no one-size-fits-all model for the family office. Every family enterprise ecosystem is unique and constantly changing and evolving. Each family has specific circumstances and needs which influence the type of family office that might work best.

While each family office is unique, there are archetypal forms of family offices that have gained significance over the years. We will now introduce the main archetypes of the family office that exist today, which may provide a guiding framework for your own journey, to ultimately help you choose the right family office type for your circumstances. Later in the book, when we discuss the structure for your family office, we will go deeper into these various archetypes, including the pros and cons of each archetype as well as the factors that you should take into account when deciding on the most suitable one for you and your family.

SINGLE FAMILY OFFICE (SFO)	MULTI FAMILY OFFICE (MFO)	HYBRID / VIRTUAL FAMILY OFFICE
Family office that has been set up by one family to take care of their specific needs	A family office that is set up to simultaneously serve multiple, typically unrelated, families	Uberization of the family office! An ecosystem-type approach where the needs of the family are served by a network of providers, and where they do not need to "own" everything themselves

SFO

Started by, and serves one family (or one branch within a wider family)

Single "Multi" Family Office

Started by, and serves multiple (or all) branches of a wider family

Closed, family-owned MFO

Started by multiple families, serving their needs, exclusively

Independent, commercial MFO

Started by one family (or professionals) which evolved to serve multiple families

Dependent, commercial MFO

Started by a bank, lawyer, etc. to serve multiple families

The Single Family Office (SFO)

This is a family office that has been created by one family to manage its own wealth and affairs, or the needs of one branch of a larger family.

Within this category, we see variations, such as what we call a *single "multi" family office*, which is founded by and serves multiple branches of a wider family. While there are many shared activities and services, it also offers tailored services branch-by-branch, such as tailored asset allocation or philanthropy, depending on the setup. This can be seen as a hybrid structure that combines some of the benefits of a single family office with the benefits of a multi family office (*see next definition*). Keeping it within the same family, while allowing each branch to consider customized services that might not overlap with the needs and wishes of other branches in the wider family, has its advantages.

The Multi Family Office (MFO)

This is a family office that has been set up to serve multiple, typically unrelated families.

Within this category, there are also variations. One is what we call the *closed, family-owned multi family office*, which is established by several unrelated families from the beginning and serves their needs exclusively. These might be families that are in business together or trust each other well enough to embark on such a joint venture.

Another form of a multi family office is the *independent, commercial multi family office*, which is started by one family but evolves to serve several unrelated families. The Rockefeller's family office is one such example, which was set up as a single family office and then built on its knowledge and expertise to become a multi family office serving many affluent families around the world.

Finally, there is what we call a *dependent or commercial multi family office*, which is brought to life by a bank or a professional services firm (a legal or fiduciary firm, for example) to serve multiple clients / families.

The Hybrid Family Office

The family-office-as-a-service, or "uberization" of the family office, is a recent phenomenon that draws on the flexibility and benefits of the global, digital economy to develop a network style approach to serving the needs of families. This involves a small team determining what services are core to the family, and deciding what the family will manage in-house and what services and talents can be outsourced or "rented" as required. The hybrid approach requires centralized management, oversight, and integration of the internal and external service providers.

We see a clear trend in the direction of hybrid family offices today. This shift is fundamentally reshaping the landscape of family offices. The hybrid family office overcomes some of the key challenges that single family offices face today, which we will be elaborating on in more detail in the organization chapter. We believe this form of family office will continue to gain popularity. However, it requires the family to have a close grip over the network of service providers to ensure that everything is working towards the same goal. Oftentimes, families conserve a smaller core team in-house that ensures that the family purpose is clear and that all partners and services are aligned with it.

The evolution of the family office

No matter what model you start from or what direction you set off in, your family office will evolve over time. This is, in part, because you will go through a learn-by-doing process that leads to finetuning or even a pivot and, in part, because the needs of your family and your environment will change over time.

For many families, the family office starts in a rather informal way. Oftentimes when we speak with families and ask them if they have a family office, they answer "kind of" or "in some way, yes", which is indicative of the fluid nature of the family office. Perhaps, at one point in time, the patriarch / matriarch of the family asks the chief financial officer of the company to take on the management of some financial affairs of the family. This may have led to the need for more family responsibilities to be managed in a professional way, leading to a more formal structure and the creation of an embedded single family office. As we saw with the Rockefellers, this single family might even expand over time into a multi family office serving the needs of many families.

For other families, the family office might take on a more formal, legal structure from the beginning as the result of the triggering event, such as the sale of the family business where there is an immediate need for an organized and professional way to manage the liquid assets that are suddenly available to the family.

When we ask principals about the origins of their family offices we often hear that these entities did not explicitly start as a family office, but rather served a specific need (such as being a holding company over some side businesses or as a mechanism to bundle the shares of one branch of the family), and that it then evolved into more of a family office over time, with the family repurposing it later on. Oftentimes they would only later call this entity a family office.

The evolution towards a more formal and professional structure that handles the total family wealth spectrum is rarely a linear process. It's a moving target that involves continuous development and adjustment to the changing needs of the family.

It is advisable to have a structured approach to re-assess the purpose and strategy of your family office in regular intervals (e.g., every 5 years, with a rolling strategic plan), just like you would in any other business. In addition, there are certain major inflection points in the life of the family enterprise ecosystem – such as generational transitions or major liquidity events – where it makes sense to do a more holistic review of the overall purpose and direction of the family office and to chart a new course for the future.

We encourage you to imagine your experience with the family office as an ongoing, lifelong learning journey, which needs to be treated as much a part of your planning and evolution as your family's personal and commercial interests.

THE FAMILY OFFICE NAVIGATOR

Based on decades of research and practice by experts from IMD Business School and the Cambridge Family Enterprise Group, and based on a global study on different identities and patterns of family offices which was conducted in partnership with the Family Business Network, the *Family Office Navigator* is an easy-to-use tool that will empower you to take ownership of all the decisions and actions necessary to design and manage an impactful family office.

The *Family Office Navigator* is structured into two main parts, which are further sub-divided into different building blocks that you and your family can work on throughout the book. The following chart provides a visual overview of the *Navigator*, which also represents the structure of the book.

Your Family Office Strategy House

The purpose of your family office (Chapter 3)

Why your family office exists and how it can help you manage the present and prepare for the aspirational future.

The focus of your family office (Chapter 4)

Defining the different services that you and your family wish the family office to provide, based on the various complexities you have identified in the "Charting your Course" chapter.

The organization of the family office (Chapter 5)

Mapping out the foundations of your family office covering areas such as the structure, resources and governance of your family offices as well as how you can ensure the effectiveness and efficiency of your family office through proper monitoring.

Your Family Enterprise Ecosystem (Chapter 2)

Charting the course for your family office
Assessing where you and your family are today (status quo) and where you and your family want to go (aspirational future).

Your family manifesto
Defining the greater purpose and values of your family and laying out the foundation for what you wish to achieve as a family.

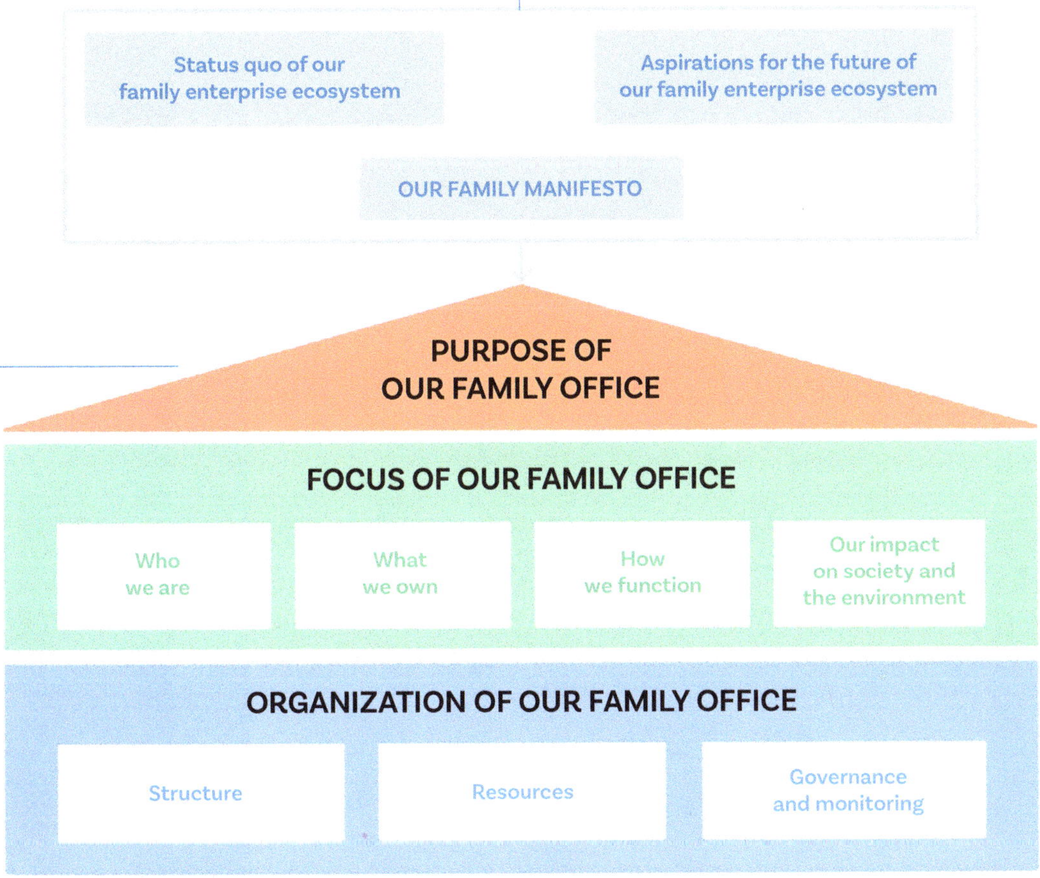

Status quo of our
family enterprise ecosystem

Aspirations for the future of
our family enterprise ecosystem

OUR FAMILY MANIFESTO

**PURPOSE OF
OUR FAMILY OFFICE**

FOCUS OF OUR FAMILY OFFICE

Who
we are

What
we own

How
we function

Our impact
on society and
the environment

ORGANIZATION OF OUR FAMILY OFFICE

Structure

Resources

Governance
and monitoring

Learning architecture (Chapter 6)
We conclude with a chapter on learning architecture, encouraging you and your family to think about how you and your family can embed learning into your core strategic approach. The goal is for you to ensure that you critically reflect on the past, on an ongoing basis, to improve the effectiveness and efficiency of your family office over time.

How to use the Family Office Navigator

We have designed the *Navigator* to be as flexible and easy to use as possible. There is no "right" way to read or use it, but we humbly suggest that you follow one of the two following paths:

1. **From start to finish**: Read each of the sections and chapters in the order we have presented them in and work through each step and task carefully, either on your own or with selected members of your family, to create a holistic vision of your custom-made family office. This route is especially targeted at those families who are considering setting up a family office or formalizing an informal and ad hoc "family office" service that is currently embedded in the family enterprise ecosystem.

2. **Go modular**: We have written each section and chapter to make it possible for you to dive into areas that are more relevant for you without missing out on essential knowledge elsewhere. This means that if you have already established the purpose of your family office or have an existing family office, but want to fine-tune your structure or organization, you can do so by going straight to the relevant parts of the *Navigator*.

One practical way to utilize the *Family Office Navigator* is to download the navigator framework from our dedicated book page on **www.imd.org/fon**. Print it out in A2 or A1 and start co-creating your family office with your family. You could utilize post-it notes to stay flexible and turn this discussion into a proper workshop.

On the right side you can find a simplified version of the *Family Office Navigator* framework for illustration purposes.

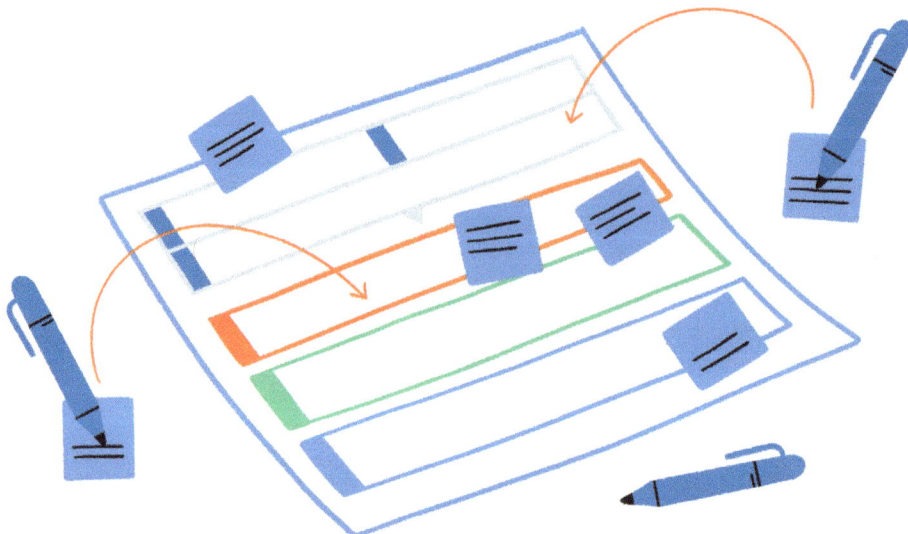

Family Office Navigator

STATUS QUO
What does our family enterprise ecosystem look like today?

ASPIRATIONAL FUTURE
What does our ideal future family enterprise ecosystem look like? Where do we want to go, together?

FAMILY MANIFESTO
What is our purpose? What are our values? What is keeping us together into the future?

FAMILY VISION / PURPOSE

FAMILY GLUE

FAMILY VALUES

PURPOSE OF OUR FAMILY OFFICE
How will our family office help us manage the present and prepare for the future of our family enterprise ecosystem?

FOCUS OF OUR FAMILY OFFICE
What are the core activities and services of our family office?

WHO WE ARE
Services to help our family members flourish & blossom and help our family stay united and harmonious

WHAT WE OWN
Services to help us manage assets, liabilities and cash flow within our family enterprise ecosystem

HOW WE FUNCTION
Services to help us ensure effective and cohesive governance and decision-making in our family enterprise ecosystem

OUR ROLE IN SOCIETY AND OUR IMPACT ON THE ENVIRONMENT
Services to help us ensure that we have the most positive impact on society and the environment

ORGANIZATION OF OUR FAMILY OFFICE
How will we be organizing our family office to ensure that it can fulfill its purpose?

STRUCTURE
What type of family office do we wish to establish and where?

RESOURCES
What resources do we need? How do we finance the family office? What is the right legal and ownership model?

GOVERNANCE
How do we govern the family office? How will we connect the family office with other mechanisms in the system?

MONITORING
How do we monitor the family office performance? What are our metrics of success?

LEARNING
What are our mechanisms for learning and for adjusting the course, if necessary?

Navigating the Navigator

The *Family Office Navigator* tool is arranged in a number of building blocks that focus on and explore the key elements of your journey towards a successful family office: charting your course, defining your purpose, deciding on the focus areas, and organizing your family office. These blocks contain key questions that address the why, what, who and how of a family office; an approach that we have found very useful in our work with hundreds of families worldwide to deliver the clarity, breadth and detail needed on this crucial journey.

The book replicates the structure of the navigator framework in a series of chapters and sections, laid out in a uniform style and pattern, to make your journey as familiar and intuitive as possible.

Each building block in the *Navigator* has its own dedicated section in the book with an introduction that outlines key questions and context, a number of carefully selected strategic choices that will clarify and inform your thinking, and practical activities to help you and your family work together to define your choices and answers to the key questions. You will also find insights boxes that are scattered throughout the book which offer you different perspectives, insights, learnings, to dos, calls to action or things to keep in mind. Finally, we have selected a series of case studies with testimonies from families around the world, describing and explaining their own approach to the family office, to provide real world examples and to share challenges and stories of success as an inspiration for your own journey. In the following we will briefly elaborate on each of these elements in a bit more detail.

- **Strategic Choices**: Through our work with enterprising families from a vast range of backgrounds and cultures, we have highlighted a vast array of strategic choices that we believe are fundamental for families to reflect on as they develop their own family office. These are effectively key decisions you and your family need to take along the way. There is no right or wrong answer to any of these. But it is essential that you come up with your own "recipe" and set of ingredients for your family office with these different options in mind. In this book, we present these strategic choices in a visual way, as a spectrum of choices across a dial or diagram of different approaches. We then pose questions to trigger discussion and debate for you and family to narrow down your options. Here is an example of such a strategic choice taken from the "Focus" chapter:

| IN-HOUSE | ←——•—•—•—•—•—•—•—•—→ | OUTSOURCED |

Managing services from within the family office

Outsourcing services to partners outside the family office

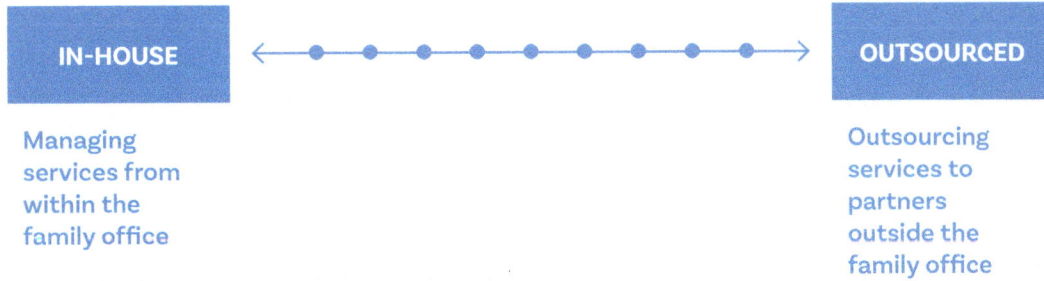

These strategic choices are designed to facilitate the conversations that are required to make informed, collective decisions about your family office. We recommend that you make time as a family and individually to reflect on each strategic choice before agreeing on a way forward.

- **Activities**: As part of the preparation and self-exploration necessary to develop an effective and suitable family office, we have found that it is highly beneficial for families and individual family members to take part in specially designed activities. These simple and practical exercises offer meaningful and engaging ways to bring the family together to discuss and gain clarity on the fundamental topics, as well as providing individuals an opportunity to reflect on the big questions at the heart of any family office decision. Consider these activities as the acid test for your choices as you move through the *Navigator*.

- **Insights from the field**: The strategic choices and activities that explore each building block of the *Navigator* will help you make clear decisions as a family. From time to time, however, you will also see "Insights from the field" boxes scattered across the chapters. We use these boxes to point out specific challenges, anecdotes from research or practice, and expert guidance that we feel is important to bear in mind. They do not require specific actions, but we recommend taking some time to reflect on each box before you make any decisions.

- **Case studies**: Before settling on a way forward, it always helps to see how other families approach and manage challenges around the family office. We have distilled the learnings and insights from interviews conducted with families and their family office staff, to offer inspiration and examples of the way different kinds of families have approached either setting up their own family office or finetuning their existing model. One aspect that we have looked at is how family offices develop over time and how they are adapting to the changing circumstances of families and family enterprise ecosystems across generations. For privacy reasons we have agreed with the families we interviewed to keep their insights anonymous.

Learning

While the core building blocks of the *Navigator* are fundamental to a rewarding journey with your family office, we cannot overemphasize the importance of continuous learning as a key pillar in this adventure.

We have created a dedicated part of this book to focus on how to learn as you go, from periodic reflections and stock-taking at each of the Navigator building blocks, to exercises and questionnaires that are designed to help you assess your progress and make the necessary adjustments.

The key to an effective and sustainable family office lies in your ability to measure progress, learn from your mistakes and successes and your willingness to make changes to your chosen course of action.

Enjoy the journey

The *Family Office Navigator* is not just a tool, it is a platform and opportunity for your family to come together and make collective, informed choices about your family office in an enjoyable, hands-on and open way.

We encourage you to involve your family in this journey, perhaps by arranging workshops with the *Navigator* tool. You may want to print out the exercises to fill out as a group, to engage each decision-maker and to inspire new ideas, cohesion and collaboration.

Decisions around family resources can often raise tensions or bring out differences of opinion. The *Navigator* offers an interactive and easy-to-use pathway to discuss sensitive issues, find middle ground and support clear, collective decisions.

It is our hope that the *Navigator* will bring your family closer together and foster understanding, while also enabling you to make the right choices.

Please do not hesitate to get in touch with us if you have any questions, reach an impasse in your discussions or need some impartial guidance.

For now, as your pilots on this journey, we look forward to sharing our practical experiences and research with you to help you design a family office that will help your family prosper and thrive into the future.

You've learned the ropes of the *Navigator* and met your crew.

Let's begin the journey.

CHAPTER 2

CHARTING YOUR COURSE

What does your current family enterprise ecosystem look like and what are your aspirations for the future?

FUTURE

«In order to know where you're going, you need to know where you're coming from.»

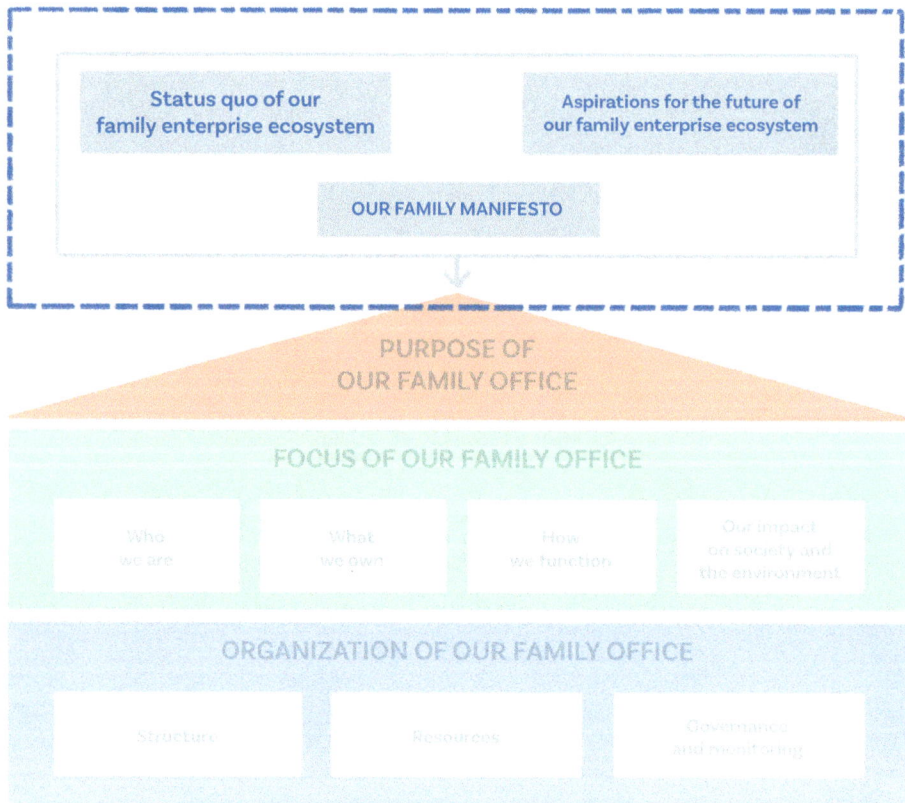

INTRODUCTION

Before we go into the specifics of the *Family Office Navigator* in the next chapter, we would like to invite you and your family to take a step back and look around you.

What does your family enterprise ecosystem look like today? Is it large or small? Is it close-knit or spread out? What is the range of activities that you and your family are involved in? Do you still have your legacy business? What is your asset situation today? What makes up your total family wealth? How simple or complex is your overall setup from the perspective of your family, business, ownership, and wealth? How do you see your family's role in society? What about its impact on the environment? Are you going through some form of transformation as a family? Has a significant event happened recently? Where do you see the biggest changes in your family enterprise ecosystem over the coming years, decades, or generations? What is your aspirational future state of your family enterprise ecosystem?

In essence, where are you today, where are you going, and what are you building?

Current state of your family enterprise ecosystem

- Who are we as a family?
- What do we own?
- How are we organized?
- What is our role in society and our impact on the environment?

Aspirational future of your family enterprise ecosystem

- What do we want our family enterprise ecosystem to be doing and look like in the future?
- What will be the most likely major / transformational changes in our ecosystem?

These are critical questions that you and your family should answer to understand whether, and what kind of, a family office is the right vehicle to help you manage the present and successfully navigate your family enterprise ecosystem into the future.

Establishing a new family office or transforming an existing family office is a critical and typically once-in-a-lifetime event for a family. It is, therefore, important to carefully plan this step, as you would any other significant life event, to ensure that you have considered all the options before you move ahead.

Every family is unique, and so is their family enterprise ecosystem. Consequently, family offices will also take on unique shapes and identities. While many of the ingredients will be the same for different families, it is difficult to create universal recipes that work for all families. This makes this reflection and assessment stage even more crucial for a successful journey, so that you can design the most appropriate model for your family office.

You are most likely considering setting up or transforming your family office because of one of the trigger events or transitional moments we highlighted in the *Introduction* of the book. Perhaps you are selling (part of or all of) the family business, considering investing assets outside of your business in order to diversify, or thinking about the best way to preserve your legacy and how a family office might help. These are significant life events or evolutions that inevitably spark big questions about our lives, our families, and our future. It is important to embrace those questions now, and to resist the urge to race ahead.

The family office as part of a life-changing moment

The trigger events or transitions that lead families to create or redesign a family office are often some of life's defining moments, with the power to influence both your short- and long-term prosperity as a family and the wellbeing of your family ecosystem.

It is unlikely that you are thinking about setting up a family office or changing an existing one out of the blue without, for example, a trigger event or some kind of newly emerged complexity driving that exploration.

It is, therefore, of paramount importance for you to understand the full implications of this transitional moment before making decisions about your family office.

To illustrate this, let's look in depth at a few of the examples we highlighted in the "Introduction". Try to imagine your own family is going through the same experience and think about the long-term implications beyond the immediate need to address this issue. Evidently, there are many more examples, but we want to walk you through some of the more common examples that we see.

The liquidity event

Let's imagine your family has recently experienced a liquidity event such as the sale of the family business. This has resulted in the release of liquidity – a percentage of which family members have agreed to jointly invest. The proceeds need to be collectively managed, and a family office seems like a reasonable solution. The obvious question to ask is what to do with the money. Of course, that question is important and must be addressed. However, there is a bigger picture here that cannot be ignored and that forces us to consider deeper questions that will influence our next steps. The sale of the family business is not just about releasing funds; it is the end of an era and a transformational moment for the family. For many families, their business is the glue that binds them together with a shared purpose and attendant occasions, such as shareholder or family assembly meetings, to meet up. Without this glue, what is the new family identity and what does the future look like? What does the family want to be now that the business has gone? Does it want to remain closely bound by a newly defined common purpose or do the different members of the family want to go separate ways? Are the ties between family members strong enough that there is a desire to stay together? What would that look like? What would they do together? Can the money from the sale of the business be used to keep the family together in some way? What kind of investment strategy would support that?

You can see that by taking the conversation one step further than wealth management, we can find greater clarity to inform the decisions that will shape the future of your family and its family office. It is important that families devote the necessary time for meaningful conversations around their values, their identity and purpose, as well as how they imagine their future now that their circumstances have changed.

Separation of certain family affairs from the legacy business

In the beginning, it is common for a family's wealth to be highly concentrated in its operating business. This is normal because, in the early phase of a business, the family knows its industry and operations intimately, and people like to invest in what they know and trust. Sometimes the family asks company employees to help the founder or family members with personal projects (e.g., tax preparation, financial advice, family meeting planning). However, at a certain point, the family will likely want to separate these activities from the business and begin to diversify their assets outside of their operating company to spread their risk. This is the point when many families look at setting up a family office to manage their private affairs away from the business. But it is not just a matter of moving assets or responsibilities around between different legal structures. A deeper reflection is required. Why is the family separating its personal activities and some financial assets from the business? What is the goal? Is it to achieve a degree of privacy, perhaps, or to better address the needs of the family, or to de-risk and diversify the investments? Has compliance required it? From a financial perspective, what is the family trying to achieve through a distinct pool of assets? Is it to ensure the family can prosper independently beyond the fate of the business? What assets and services will need to be separated? What are the needs of the family?

Again, addressing these types of deeper questions generates valuable information for the shaping the role of the family office.

Increased family complexity

As families evolve, it is inevitable that their ecosystems become more complex. Over generations, the enterprising family grows in size and diversity and its members pursue different dreams in different corners of the world. While the family business has served as the glue that keeps the family together, there are different centrifugal forces at work, pulling the family apart. The proportion of actively involved family members decreases, ownership becomes diluted and unevenly distributed over generations, and the emotional bond to the legacy business typically declines.

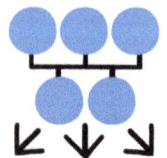

INNER CORE OF THE FAMILY
Family members that are actively involved (as shareholders, in different operational or governance roles, etc.)

OUTER CORE OF THE FAMILY
Family members that attend meetings and are involved in other activities, but not in a leading operational or governance role

PERIPHERY OF THE FAMILY
Family members that are more distant to / not involved in the business, governance roles and family activities

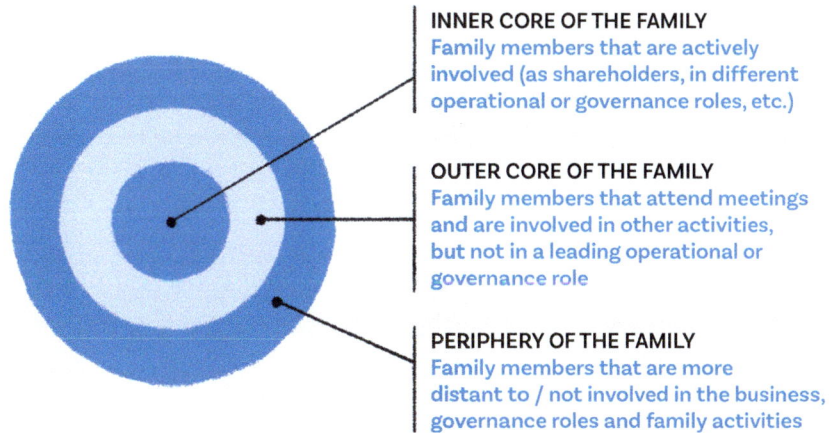

This evolution could call for the creation or fine-tuning of a family office structure to take care of the family's diverse needs. When aspects of our lives become more complex, it is not always easy to understand how to design the right solution, especially without serious reflection. In these circumstances, families can struggle to really know what needs they have and how a family office can help them.

All the more reason, therefore, to ask some big questions. What is the family trying to achieve and what support does it need to make that happen? How is the next generation being engaged and encouraged to contribute to the family enterprise? Is it time to think about talent development (for roles inside and outside of the business) as a strategic priority for the success of the family enterprise? Does that mean investing in specific education for family members or the creation of a dedicated seed fund to support family entrepreneurship? What about family governance? How are family members kept informed, given a platform for sharing opinions, or involved in decision-making? As family members move geographically further away from the epicenter of the business, how will the family remain connected to the company and to other family members? How will tax and inheritance plans shift as a result of geographic mobility? If there are no family members working inside the company, how will the family steer and oversee the company from other positions? Without knowing the answer to these broader questions, it is difficult for a family to design a family office to respond effectively to its increased complexity.

While there are no silver bullet solutions or perfect blueprints, you should reflect on the trigger event(s) or transitional moment(s) that have led you here and approach the decisions that will shape your family office in a deliberate manner. In other words, you need to do your homework.

Activity 1 at the end of the "Purpose" chapter will guide you through the reflection process as a family with respect to the different trigger events and what the implications might be with respect to your family office.

While it is true that most family offices are set up, at least in the initial phase, to handle the financial affairs of the family, it is a mistake to assume that money management is the only issue you need to or can address. It is strongly advisable to take some time in the beginning to reflect and engage in some critical conversations as a family to understand the status quo of your entire family enterprise ecosystem and your aspirations for the future.

From our observations working with diverse families around the world, once engaged in this meaningful reflection, families enjoy and benefit greatly from the experience of delving deeper into these questions to fully explore the best way forward.

For families with existing family offices

Your family enterprise ecosystem is a constantly evolving living world, influenced by internal and external factors and actors. As such, it is essential that your family office also evolves to adapt to the changing nature of this ecosystem and to ensure that it is serving the family in the most effective and efficient way. You and your family should regularly review and assess the key dimensions of your family enterprise ecosystem – who you are, what you own, how you are organized, your role in society, and where you wish to go – to provide the necessary direction to your family officers. Without this regular reflection and assessment, there is a risk that your family office and the people that manage it will drift off track or that decisions will be taken based on conversations that happened in the past, possibly leading to suboptimal results.

By suboptimal, we do not necessarily only refer to financial returns, but in a more holistic sense whether the family office helps you preserve and nurture your overall family enterprise ecosystem and manage your family's total wealth. What is important to keep in mind is that family office managers perform best if they have clear guidance from the family in terms of what they wish to achieve with their family office and what success means for you and your family.

Effective family officers can play a key role in helping families design their overall ownership strategy and can help to put in place the proper governance across all aspects of your family enterprise ecosystem to ensure that the family office is performing at its best.

We appreciate the fact that, for some of you, it might be a challenging, possibly even impossible task, at this stage to think about big questions such as the aspirational future for your family enterprise ecosystem. You might just have gone through a stressful liquidity event and simply want to get going and figure out the best way to manage your assets in the short run.

Unfortunately, many families who are just at the beginning of their family office journey – especially if there was a sudden liquidity event – dive headfirst into the water for fear of missing out on attractive investment opportunities. However, without proper upfront reflection about the purpose and aspirations of the family, there is a heightened risk of hasty decisions, poor strategy formulation and the creation of an inadequate structure in this early stage.

Here are some of the mistakes that we see families make at this early stage.

Insights from the field: Mistakes made in haste

From our perspective, embracing the big picture reflection that accompanies the "family office conversation" is a necessary and natural part of the journey. Here are some classic mistakes that families make as a result of rushing ahead without engaging in a deeper conversation.

Hiring a CEO for your family office too quickly

Some families do not want to get involved personally in the design or setup of their family office. They want a quick fix, a hassle-free solution to address some key areas, in the hope that someone else will take care of everything. Usually, this means hiring someone to do all the work on their behalf – and finding that person quickly. Unfortunately, this tends to lead to the family appointing the wrong kind of professional for their needs or, even worse, becoming dependent on an individual or firm who has designed the family office according to their own preferences, rather than the requirements of the family.

Insourcing too many functions to the family office

When families hurry the process of setting up or updating a family office after a major event or transition, it is tempting to fall into the trap of building too many in-house capabilities within the family office, an approach which may not be strategic since many capabilities would perhaps be better sourced from the market. Rushing forward can drive up operational costs and create a bloated, inefficient family office structure that does not deliver the best value or impact.

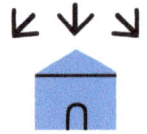

Lack of proper family office governance

Once a professional individual or team has been put in place to run the family office, some families lose interest in the operational side of the office and assume it is in safe hands. The risk is that the family loses control over what the family office delivers and manages for them. In turn, we see the mission drift – an unfortunate situation where the family office fails to keep up with the evolving needs of the family.

First investments

Families who establish a new family office can make some costly mistakes when it comes to their first investments. Either because they were rushing into it, searching for investment opportunities without clarity on their key performance indicators (KPIs), or they were approached by someone with an investment proposal and did not conduct the appropriate due diligence. Affluent families, especially after a liquidity event that has caught the public's attention (e.g., a business has been sold or listed on the stock market), are often the targets of unsolicited investment offerings. Not knowing how to assess them can lead to costly errors.

Picking the best-known multi-family office

We have all fallen into the trap of buying something based on the brand, only to realize there might have been a much better option, if we had just spent some time doing our research. In the same way, it is easy to be impressed by a well-established multi-family office that already has a big reputation or provides services to successful families and / or your peers. This does not automatically mean they are the right fit for your family.

Going with the "friend" who seems to know it all

Some entrepreneurs or families enter into an agreement with a close friend or another family to collaborate or join forces. Oftentimes, these types of arrangements are made because one party does not feel fit to manage / oversee the family office or has no or little interest in financial matters. These arrangements are rather informal and rely on the trust and good relationship that exists between two or more individuals. However, when a generational transition occurs, the close ties and the tacit knowledge of this symbiotic relationship are often not desirable for the next generation. Families can end up in a poorly structured or badly governed setup with partners they do not know very well, which might prove costly to either exit from or restructure professionally.

Leaving it to the one leader of the family

Families are made up of individuals - each with their own strengths, capabilities, and interests. It is natural that some individuals are more interested in, or familiar with financial matters and investments than others. Since family offices are seen as something rather technical and the initial focus of the family office is often on investments, families tend to delegate this task to the person with the most interest or experience in this domain. However, entrusting the task to one family member poses the risk of a disconnect or a growing divide between the one actively involved individual (or small group of individuals) and the rest of the family and ownership group. It is of utmost importance that the "chosen leader" creates an inclusive atmosphere and process to ensure that everybody from the family can be involved in establishing the family office. Otherwise, the delegation approach can backfire later on in the process.

Making mistakes is human; it is part of life and part of every new venture activity. Setting up a family office is, effectively, an entrepreneurial undertaking and it is natural that you will make some mistakes. While you will not be able to avoid making mistakes, it is important that you lay the foundation to avoid the costliest mistakes in the beginning while you and your family are learning. We will return to this concept of learning several times throughout the book because we believe it is the most essential aspect of this journey.

To support you in the crucial step of assessing where you are, why you are here, and where you want to go, in this chapter and its related activities section, we will first guide you through a series of questions and exercises that will help you map out your family enterprise ecosystem as it is today. Activity 1 at the end of this chapter will enable you to understand the true nature of your current circumstances, with all its complexities, challenges and assets.

From there, Activity 2 will help you work out where you want to go with your family office by contemplating your aspirational goals as a family across the spectrum of your total family wealth. And, finally, for those families that have not already agreed on their collective values and / or written a family manifesto - or for those of you who want to update either of those aspect - Activity 3 and Activity 4 offer a clear path to support those important processes.

We call this entire stage "charting your course" – the vital preparation any traveler needs to undertake before embarking on a journey into unknown territories.

Only then can we move on, with confidence, to consider what the purpose and focus of your family office will be and how to manage its organizational structure to bring it all to life.

No matter what has led you to think about a family office at this point in time or how simple or complex your family enterprise ecosystem is, this chapter will help you define a vision for the future and develop a clear idea about what your family office needs to do and why.

Once you have completed this chapter, you will have:

- ☑ An informed understanding of your current situation, your total family wealth, and your family enterprise ecosystem
- ☑ A clear sense of direction about why you are here, where you want to go, and what you want to achieve
- ☑ The information needed to define the purpose of your family office and to progress with confidence and clarity to the next steps of the *Family Office Navigator*

WHAT IS THE CURRENT STATE OF YOUR FAMILY ENTERPRISE ECOSYSTEM?

In the previous chapter, we introduced the concepts of the family enterprise ecosystem and total family wealth. Here's a quick refresher:

> - **Family enterprise ecosystem**: a dynamic and evolving system that includes all aspects related to the family, the businesses and other assets that the family owns, the way in which you govern the family, ownership, businesses and wealth, as well as your role in society and impact on the environment.
> - **Total family wealth**: Human, social, financial, reputational, intellectual, and other forms of capital, representing the overall wealth of a family enterprise ecosystem beyond just its financial means.

We will be using these terminologies throughout the book, and they are important concepts to grasp at this stage of your family office journey because they will allow you to reflect on the present and future in a holistic way before you dive into operational matters.

In this book, we chose the visual metaphor of a coral reef because we felt that it best illustrated the complexity and beauty of an ecosystem and the fact that every ecosystem is unique. The same holds true for your family enterprise ecosystem. We want you to immerse yourself in your ecosystem, identify its treasures and assets (your total family wealth), as well as the challenges and complexities that need to be managed. Taking a wider and deeper perspective beyond your financial means enables you to explore how to shape your future across all the components that make up your ecosystem and, with it, your total family wealth.

Different stages of family enterprise ecosystems

Before we move forward to this essential "mapping" step, we would like to introduce three stage of family development. Each stage corresponds to a level of maturity and complexity of your family enterprise ecosystem. Later in the book, we will elaborate on the archetypes of family offices that best fit the needs of families in each phase, in order to illustrate different scenarios and considerations.

Most of you would probably agree that each enterprising family you meet is unique and different to yours. Therefore, it may surprise you that families and family enterprises share several common traits and challenges at various stages of their evolution. We have tracked these patterns and identified three phases of family enterprise ecosystems. We encourage you to identify your current stage and think about how that stage's characteristics influence your reflections regarding your family office.

Defining the client of the family office

As you can see from these stages, the characteristics of the family and their ecosystems vary significantly. While we will not be going into technicalities about family office structure and design at this point, it is important for you to think about who from your family will be (at least initially) the client of the family office.

While in some cases this might be obvious – for example if you are the founder of a company and had a liquidity event, then wish for the assets to be managed – it can be less obvious in others. For example, imagine you are part of a large, multi-generational family that collectively owns a business, and you just went through a major liquidity event. Your family is made up of several branches. It is possible to imagine different scenarios when it comes to who the family office clients could be:

· It could focus exclusively on your branch of the family
· It could focus on the wider family, across all branches, with centralized services and joint investment activities
· It could adopt a hybrid approach, combining generic services to the wider family while offering each branch or each family member access to bespoke services and investment opportunities
· It could be that you end up with a hybrid model whereby you and your branch build your own family office for some activities but participate (with part of your assets) in a shared family office set up for the wider family
· It could be that you and your branch end up building a family office together with other non-related families because you have a strong personal and professional connection with them

No matter what the choice, it is important to ensure that you are clear about who the initial clients of your family office will be, because you will need to include them in the discussions and activities set out in the *Family Office Navigator*.

	Typical characteristics	Some structural considerations for a family office
Founder / controlling owner stage	• Small family (often 1st or 2nd gen) • Central position of controlling owner • Leadership & governance dictated by founder / controlling owner • Little complexity in the family enterprise system • Wealth is highly concentrated in the business • Liquid wealth derived from profitable operations or liquidity event leading to sudden wealth	• Most likely a pure investment office (at least in the beginning) • Potentially a few additional custom services, depending on the particular needs and wants of the family (for example, concierge services)
Evolving / maturing family business stage	• Increasing family size (often 3rd generation onwards) • Ownership distributed across branches of the family • Family may be in operational roles or may lead only in governance and ownership roles • Increased complexity of the system, particularly regarding governance • Increased risk of conflicts (between siblings, cousins, branches,…) • Business has grown, likely diversified, sometimes reaching conglomerate stage • A large proportion of the family's assets are bound in the legacy business until a liquidity event happens • Investable wealth derived from profits from legacy operations, sale of a company, or fast-growing new ventures	• Investment office with mandate to slowly start building a portfolio of assets • Supporting the family with specific needs (e.g., education of NxG, governance, etc.) • Some additional custom services
Large / dynastic family enterprise stage	• Large family (50+ family members across multiple branches, no more distinct generations) • Large complexity of the family enterprise system • Diversified portfolio of assets • Oftentimes, the family is no longer in a leading operational role in the legacy business (if they still have one)	• Managing the family's portfolio of assets • Organizing various governance forums for the family • Supporting the family with talent development • Supporting the family with unity-building and relationship-building • Providing concierge services

Remember that a family enterprise ecosystem is constantly changing over time. Family sizes, structures, and dynamics evolve over time. Equally, a family's portfolio of businesses and its control (through leadership and / or ownership) of these businesses is always evolving. Take a few moments to reflect on the stage that you are at today. Think about the most important changes that have happened in the past and the changes that are most likely to happen in the future.

For established family offices

If you already have a family office, ask yourself the following questions to establish where you are on your journey and how you might need to reshape your family office for the future.

Past:

- Which stage did your family enterprise system resemble most when your family office was created?
- How have things evolved since then? Has something fundamentally changed over time?

Present:

- Which of the three family enterprise ecosystem stages do you identify with today?
- What has changed from the beginning until today? What has not changed?

Future:

- What aspects of your family office will have to change / evolve given this new / different stage?

Key pillars of your family enterprise ecosystem

In the "Introduction" chapter, you will remember we spoke about the "five stones" framework for a healthy family enterprise ecosystem, including the individuals in the system, the family, the ownership group, the businesses, as well as the role of your family in society and its impact on the environment. We also introduced the concept of total family wealth. For the exercise of mapping the current status of your family enterprise ecosystem, we will combine the core elements of the "five stones" framework and the total family wealth concept into four key pillars:

Who we are: this pillar looks at the individual and family level, including all family members, their overall setup, the complexity of the family system, and relationships, among other dimensions related to human and social capital.

What we own: this pillar looks at all the assets, liabilities, and cash flow within the family enterprise ecosystem, including businesses, investments, and other assets.

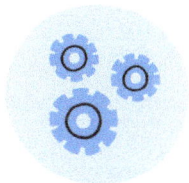

How we function: this pillar looks at the existing governance mechanisms that hold the entire ecosystem together, relating to the family, ownership, business and wealth.

Our role in society and our impact on the environment: this pillar looks at the various ESG principles and related activities that are carried out as part of the ecosystem, from transformational initiatives within the businesses to impact investment and philanthropy.

Based on our work helping families around the world design or redesign their family offices, we have developed a clear process, set out in Activity 1 at the end of this chapter, to help you and your family map out the status quo of your family enterprise ecosystem, through the lens of these four dimensions.

Going through the exercise is an important and rewarding activity. First, after completing this activity, most families end up being surprised about how vibrant and diverse their ecosystem is. Secondly, it allows families to have meaningful conversations exploring different points of views and, in some cases, identifying knowledge gaps in a structured way. It can, therefore, serve as an educational tool (to orient the next generation, for instance). Third, it is a simple way to identify weaknesses as well as hidden or neglected areas in your family enterprise ecosystem. Your family office, if you so wish, could over time become a catalyst and a platform for the sustainable and effective management of your entire family enterprise ecosystem – in other words, become the guardian, custodian, and caretaker of everything that falls within the sphere of influence of your family. At the very least, being aware of your total wealth as a family, and how its various factors interact as part of the overall ecosystem, will help you make an informed choice about what you want from your family office and how to manage it.

Before we dive into the exercise of mapping out your family enterprise ecosystem, we would like to take you on a journey into the future.

ASPIRATIONS FOR THE FUTURE OF YOUR FAMILY ENTERPRISE ECOSYSTEM

It is time for you and your family to project yourself into the future and imagine what your idealized future family enterprise system might look like. Activity 2 at the end of this chapter will serve as a structured process for you and your family to complete this task. But, first, let's explain the rationale for investing your efforts into this stage of the process.

While family offices exist to manage the present situation of your family, they can also play a crucial role in laying the foundations for a desired future. Also, the people working with you and your family in the family office can be key players in ensuring that you work together effectively towards that vision - keeping the family on track and focused on your goals. Family offices should, therefore, be designed in a way that serves families across generations. Having supported many diverse, multi-generational families on this journey, we see that the most successful and well-functioning family enterprise ecosystems embrace a multi-generational perspective.

The term "future" means different things for different people. Some might be thinking five or 10 years ahead. Some think about their children. Others think two to three generations, or more, into the future. This is totally up to you, but we generally recommend that if you are setting up a new family office, you use a 10-year time horizon. If you already have a family office, you should project out further, such as one generation (approximately 25 years). However, it is important that everybody who is involved in the process agrees on the time horizon you wish to adopt for this exercise.

Envisioning the future can begin with a series of open questions. Where do you see your family in this future scenario? What would you like your family to achieve in the near-, mid-, and long-term? Have you thought about what kind of legacy and foundation you are creating for your children and their children? Do you have specific goals for any of the dimensions of your total family wealth (developing the human, social, financial, reputational and intellectual capital of your family)? What stage will your family be in? Will you be a family in business? Will you be an entrepreneurial or investing family? Will you be doing things together across all branches of the family, or separately? Will you engage in philanthropy or impact investing? What will be your reputational capital in your community and beyond?

Visualizing your family enterprise ecosystem and total family wealth

Let's return to the image of the coral reef to help illustrate your family enterprise ecosystem and your total family wealth. We invite you to see all the beautiful living creatures, colors, shapes and form as metaphors for your family enterprise ecosystem.

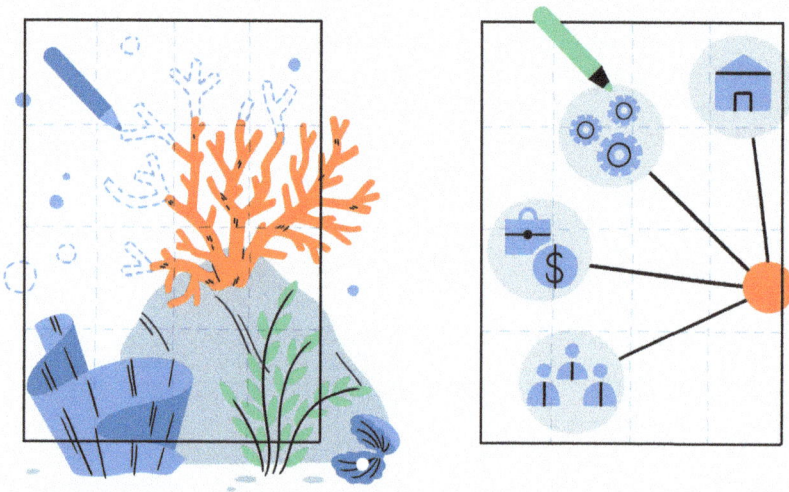

Your future coral reef (metaphor)	Your future family enterprise ecosystem
Will your future coral reef... • Look similar to what it looks like today? • Have evolved, grown, or diversified over time? • Have become more colorful with new creatures and species living in it? • Have split up to form several different, smaller coral reefs?	• Will your family look similar to what it looks like today (similar geography, family proximity, interests and activities, for example)? • Will you still be active in the same business, focusing on its health and growth? • Will you have enriched your family enterprise ecosystem with new business activities that you founded, invested in or acquired, or with new activities such as a family office, philanthropy or family events? • Will different parts of your family have gone their own way to focus on their own activities or on their nuclear families to create their own legacy?

We appreciate that a far-reaching exercise might feel overwhelming for some individuals and families at this stage in time. Maybe you just sold your legacy business and want to figure out, as quickly as possible, what you could do with the money. Or you might still have very young children and feel like you are not ready to think about topics such as succession and multi-generational issues.

However, we strongly recommend that, no matter where you are in your journey, you take some time to map out your desired future, even if this future is years ahead. In our experience, it is sensible and natural to engage with these questions before establishing a family office (or before considering the redesign of an existing family office). Not only will they help you understand the implications of the trigger or transitional event, they will also help you make the most appropriate choices in the set-up stage of your family office.

The course has been charted

Once you have completed this chapter, you and your family should have a clear understanding of the state of your family enterprise ecosystem and total family wealth, including all the treasures in your coral reef and the distinct aspects that you might want a family office to take care of.

If appropriate, you will also have reflected on, explored, and fleshed out a vision of the future for your family, which in turn will inform your reflection as to whether and how a family office can best serve your family now and in the future.

With the passing of time and the coming of new generations, these circumstances will inevitably change, and your needs and goals will evolve. But an initial understanding of your starting point and desired destination will help you take off in the right direction. It will also make it easier to revisit the process to adjust your direction of travel. As with any new venture, the most important thing is to take the first step.

It is now time to go through a series of activities that will help you go through this important step in a structured way.

ACTIVITIES

We recommend undertaking this part of your journey by gathering the key members of your family together to reflect on the status quo and the future in a holistic, collaborative way. This is not a one-off decision for one individual; it is a living and breathing endeavor that you are embarking on together. If your children are too young to have a say, then take this step with your partner or spouse, or with other key family members who can contribute to a strategic brainstorming session and who may become a part of – or a client of – the family office in the future.

The setting in which you approach these reflections matters too. We recommend that you and your family take some time off and find somewhere quiet and inspiring, outside your everyday environment. The process should not be handled in between emails and meetings at the office. It is much too important for that. Invest in the process and focus on instilling a positive spirit into the reflection workshop.

It might be helpful to seek professional facilitation in what can be a challenging conversation. This would also allow all family members to be participants rather than needing one person to act as a moderator or facilitator. You might want to take a long weekend as a family and combine some of these reflective exercises with some family fun and leisure.

The reflection will take time. Committing to the exploration process might not be possible for some families in special circumstances (for instance, if everyone is scattered across the globe and busy with their own lives). Yet making this an inclusive process that brings in the wider family, rather than having one (or a few) family members working through it "on behalf of the family" will pay off in the long run as it builds emotional ownership.

Remember this is a journey. We recommend you embrace this moment as an opportunity to strengthen family engagement, to share and crystallize your family's ambitions. The more you invest in this process now, the easier the next steps in your journey will be.

> **Family Office Navigator questions:**
>
> - What does our family enterprise ecosystem look like today?
> - What does our ideal future family enterprise ecosystem look like? Where do we want to go, together?
> - What is our purpose? What are our values? What is keeping us together into the future?

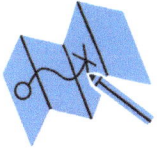

ACTIVITY 1:
MAPPING THE CURRENT STATE OF YOUR FAMILY ENTERPRISE SYSTEM

The first assessment activity for you and your family is to map the current state of your family enterprise ecosystem across the four pillars we outlined earlier in this chapter:

1. **Who are we as a family?**
2. **What do we own?**
3. **How do we function?**
4. **What is our role in society and our impact on the environment?**

This exercise will lead you to understand the level of complexity of your family enterprise, which then lays the foundation for a later discussion about which family office services are the right fit for you.

Step 1:
Complete the questionnaire

Complete the following set of questions to create a general understanding of the state of your family enterprise ecosystem.

This is a wonderful group exercise to do together at a family meeting because answering these questions likely requires the collective intelligence and insights of different family members to arrive at meaningful answers. If your family is not experienced in structuring group conversations that combine different opinions to reach a consensus, ask family members to complete the questionnaire individually first, and then share and discuss your responses together. You could also invite an outside facilitator to guide the exercise.

While this activity might seem trivial for family members who are actively involved in day-to-day leadership or governance matters, it can prove challenging and even eye-opening for those family members who do not have an active role in the system, such as the next generation or less active shareholders. As such, it offers a valuable opportunity to share information and educate the wider family about the nature of your ecosystem.

Questionnaire

WHO ARE WE AS A FAMILY?

Who do we consider as part of our enterprising family?

What is the size of our family?
- ____ (lineal descendants)
- ____ (in-laws)
- ____ (total number of living family members)

Who founded our legacy business (considered "generation 1")?

Which generation is currently in charge:
- of operations: ____
- of governance: ____
- of ownership (voting): ____

Where does family life predominantly take place, from a geographical standpoint?

Do family members live close to one another or are they dispersed across the globe (different countries, time zones, legal or tax jurisdictions, etc.)?

Are family members emotionally close to one another? Are family members most attentive and supportive:
- Within their branch?
- Across branches?
- Within their generation?
- Across generations?
- What are our family values?

[Note: If you have not yet specified your family values and wish to do so, please do so with the support of Activity 3 at the end of this chapter.]

WHAT DO WE OWN?

Total financial wealth (net worth) of the family: _____

What is the family's legacy business? Do we still control it?

Do we own other businesses? Which ones? Why do we own these businesses?

How are the other businesses organized and how do we own / control them (legally)? What percentage ownership do we have in each of the businesses? Is the family still actively engaged (management / board) or passively investing in the other businesses?

What is the value of our other assets outside of the business and liquid investments (real estate, art, etc.)?

Estimated percentage of the family's joint financial wealth that is bound in:
- Operating businesses: ___ %
- Real estate: ____ %
- Liquid assets (cash, equities, cash equivalents): _____ %
- Other assets: ____ %

Is ownership of these collective assets equally distributed across the family or is ownership concentrated with some individuals or branches in the family?

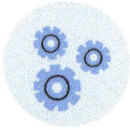

HOW DO WE FUNCTION?

What are some of the key activities that our family undertakes to foster family unity and trust? (e.g., family events, educational programs, family newsletter, etc.)

Where do our family activities and gatherings typically take place, geographically? Is this location unifying for the family?

For each of the following topics, how well do we communicate within the family and by what means?
- Information about what we own and business performance
- Changes, news, updates, timely announcements, celebrations about family or business
- When we have a perspective to share with management or the board
- When we disagree with each other inside or outside the business
- To show our appreciation and care for other family members

Which of these family governance mechanisms do we have in place?
- Family constitution / protocol (Yes / No)
- Family assembly (Yes / No)
- Family council (Yes / No)

Which of these ownership governance mechanisms do we have in place?
- Shareholder agreement (Yes / No)
- Shareholder assembly (Yes / No)
- Shareholder council (Yes / No)

What is the role and influence of the family in the business(es) – via leadership or board roles, as owners, or in other ways?

WHAT IS OUR ROLE IN SOCIETY AND OUR IMPACT ON THE ENVIRONMENT?

How do we contribute to society? Do we have a defined social mission? Have we adopted any specific approaches for achieving collective impact?

What activities do we conduct in:
- Philanthropy (family or corporate)
- Impact investment
- Corporate Social Responsibility (CSR)
- Other (please specify)

How does our family enterprise ecosystem affect the environment?

What do we do to mitigate our environmental impact?

Step 2:
Chart the complexities of your family enterprise ecosystem

Now that you have generated a high-level overview of your family enterprise ecosystem, it's time to map out the different levels of complexity within that ecosystem.

Knowing the complexity level of your system will help you identify the scope and scale of your family's needs. This understanding will, in turn, help you work out the bespoke array of services your family office ought to have in order to satisfy those needs.

We have created a simple, qualitative tool that allows you to translate the information from the preceding questionnaire into an assessment of the *complexity* of your ecosystem. For each of the four key pillars (i – iv) you analyzed in Step 1 of this activity, we have established three parameters (on a scale of 1 to 5) to estimate the complexity of each pillar within your ecosystem, whereby 1 indicates low complexity and 5 indicates high complexity.

Start by filling in this form individually. Once everybody has completed this step, each person should present and explain their answers to the family. With this information, work together to create a collective chart that illustrates the complexity of your family enterprise ecosystem.
You can either do this in a qualitative way or in a quantitative way – by adding up the scores for each pillar.

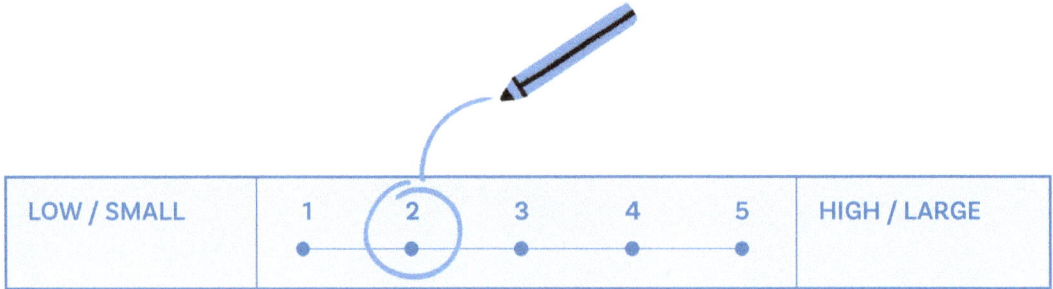

LOW / SMALL	1	2	3	4	5	HIGH / LARGE

WHO ARE WE AS A FAMILY?

< 10 Individuals	SIZE OF FAMILY The total number of living family members in our business family 1 2 3 4 5	> 50 Individuals
Family members are emotionally very close to one another	EMOTIONAL DISTANCE How close or distant, emotionally, is the wider family with each other? 1 2 3 4 5	Family members are emotionally very distant from one another
Family members are geographically very close to one another	GEOGRAPHICAL DISTANCE How close or distant, geographically, is the wider family to one another? 1 2 3 4 5	Family members are geographically very distant from one another

< 30 million USD	TOTAL FINANCIAL WEALTH	> 500 million USD
	Collectively-owned financial wealth of our family	
	1 2 3 4 5	
Our family is focused on only one business	SCOPE OF BUSINESS ACTIVITIES	Our family is involved in a large volume and / or diverse variety of different businesses, either as owner-managers or strategic investors
	Quantity and variety of different businesses that our family is involved in	
	1 2 3 4 5	
Our wealth is highly concentrated in the core business with very few other assets	SCOPE OF ASSETS OUTSIDE BUSINESSES	Our wealth is highly diversified and spread across many different assets and asset classes
	Magnitude and variety of assets that our family owns outside our core businesses	
	1 2 3 4 5	

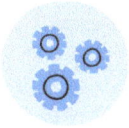

HOW DO WE FUNCTION?

Governance mechanisms are weak, ineffective, or non-existent in our family enterprise ecosystem	SOPHISTICATION OF GOVERNANCE	Highly sophisticated and established governance mechanisms across all aspects of our family enterprise ecosystem
	Level of sophistication of governance mechanisms (family, ownership, business, and investments) within our family enterprise ecosystem	
	1 2 3 4 5	

Very few or sporadic events and activities take place in our family and / or ownership group	**SCOPE OF FAMILY ACTIVITIES** The amount and variety of different events and activities of our family and ownership group 1 2 3 4 5	There is an array of different events and activities that are well established and managed
There is very little communication within our family enterprise ecosystem and it is not structured or effective	**SOPHISTICATION OF COMMUNICATION** The frequency and effectiveness of information-sharing and communication within the family enterprise ecosystem 1 2 3 4 5	There is a very well established, structured, and managed approach to communication

WHAT IS OUR ROLE IN SOCIETY AND OUR IMPACT ON THE ENVIRONMENT

We do not engage in any philanthropic activities as a family (outside of our business)	**PHILANTHROPIC ENGAGEMENT** Level and sophistication of the family's philanthropic engagement 1 2 3 4 5	We are actively engaged in philanthropy and it plays a central role in our family
We do not engage in any ESG or impact-related activities through our businesses or investments	**ESG ACTIVITIES IN BUSINESS AND INVESTMENTS** The level and sophistication of ESG- and impact-related activities as part of our businesses and investments 1 2 3 4 5	We are actively engaged in a variety of ESG and impact-related activities through our businesses and investments, and this plays a central role in our family enterprise ecosystem

Our activities are siloed. There is no coordination across our various activities in order to achieve collective impact	**COLLECTIVE IMPACT** The degree of coordination across all our CSR, impact investing, and philanthropic activities to achieve collective impact 1 2 3 4 5 ●——●——●——●——●	Our various activities are fully aligned and we have a centralized collective impact strategy and governance in place

Step 3:
Assess the "health" of your family enterprise ecosystem

Once you have finished charting your collective view of your family enterprise ecosystem, we suggest that you engage in a qualitative discussion about the health of this ecosystem. As outlined in the "Introduction" chapter, we believe that it is important that you strive to maintain the health and wellbeing of your family enterprise ecosystem across the "five stones" – the individuals in the system, the family, the ownership group, the businesses, as well as the role of your family in society and its impact on the environment.

As a family, discuss the following questions:

- How would we evaluate our system's overall "health" along the "five stones" of our family enterprise ecosystem?
- How would we evaluate the resilience and adaptability of our family enterprise ecosystem along those five dimensions?
- Where do we have major weaknesses or gaps that we should address?

ACTIVITY 2:
SKETCHING OUT YOUR ASPIRATIONS FOR THE FUTURE OF YOUR FAMILY ENTERPRISE ECOSYSTEM

As explained earlier in this chapter, this reflective exercise about your family's wishes for the future is very important. Since there is no right or wrong answer to any of the questions that follow, it is important that you (and all other family members who participate in this activity) are in the right frame of mind. You need to allow yourself the opportunity to rise above day-to-day life to think about the future.

Again, it may be worthwhile to consider the support of an expert to help facilitate this process. In practice, we have found that third party support can break the ice and help to keep conversations constructive and on track. Remember that the kind of questions and shared contemplation that you focus on at this stage will depend on the nature of the trigger event or transitional moment that your family is facing (for instance, if you just sold your legacy business, you would have to face questions such as, "Do we want to stay together as a family? Why are we better off together than alone?"). You might be in search of a new "glue" for the family, now that the old "glue" is gone.

Step 1:
Individual reflection

Go through this first step individually, without consulting any other family members. Each family member should dedicate the necessary time to genuinely reflect on this process. Be honest and open, taking the full spectrum, nature, complexity, and health of your total family wealth and family enterprise ecosystem into account.

To inform your reflections, it will help to review your family's answers to Activity 1. We also suggest that you (a) define the timeframe you have in mind for the short-, mid- and long-term "future" (for example, five to ten years, one generation, two or more generations in the future) in order to (b) project yourself into that future and imagine what your family enterprise ecosystem will look like.

Looking at each of the key pillars from Activity 1, ask yourself: *What are the most likely changes to our family enterprise system in the short-, mid- and long-term?*

Dimension	What changes do we expect in the short-, mid- and long-term?
Who are we as a family?	
What do we own?	
How do we function?	
What is our role in society and our impact on the environment?	

Some further prompting questions

Here are some supplementary questions to help you navigate these key themes. You don't need to address all of them, but they will serve as a useful inspiration and guide.

- What aspects of the family enterprise ecosystem would have stayed essentially the same and which ones would have changed over time? What changes do you foresee in the family, your business and investment activities, your governance as well as your role in society and the environment?
- Will your family look similar to what it looks like today (e.g., similar geography, family proximity, interests, activities)?
- Will you still be active with the same business, focusing on its health and growth?
- Will you have enriched your family enterprise ecosystem with new business activities that you founded, invested in, or acquired, or with new activities such as a family office, philanthropy, or family events?
- Will different parts of your family have gone their own way to focus on their own activities and on their nuclear family to create their own legacy?
- How will our family's total wealth have changed and evolved (human, social, financial, reputational, and intellectual capital)?

At this stage, it might be useful to sketch or draw your future family enterprise ecosystem. Since this whole reflection exercise is a creative one, it also makes sense to employ creativity techniques that suit everyone. If it helps you, feel free to keep referring to the metaphor of the coral reef. You can use different colors and symbols to illustrate different parts of your ecosystem and how it might change over time. You can then also think about creating different possible scenarios, just to play around with different ideas and try to imagine what it would be like if one or the other scenario were to become reality. How would that make you feel or think about your family?

Step 2:
Collective exercise as a family

Come together as a family to share your individual reflections and ideas. One person should be a designated "note-taker" to summarize the discussions.

Step 3:
Making sense of it all as a family

Drawing on the collective discussion in Step 2, aggregate your perspectives and define a clear, collective view for your aspirational future for the family. This is an essential step because this will help to inform the choices you need to make for your future family office.

ACTIVITY 3:
OUR FAMILY VALUES

Values drive and shape your activities – whether in your family, in your business, as an investor, or in philanthropy. They help you to understand the context in which you operate and define what you want to achieve individually and as a family. This exercise will help you reflect on your core personal values as well as the values that characterize your family, and to find common ground with members of your family as you embark on your family office journey. This process can be useful to agree a set of fixed values that can serve as the moral compass for your family, to identify values that you wish to pass on to the next generation, or to refine existing values. It will also help you to understand how these values can be instrumental in selecting the kind of organization(s) you would like to partner with or invest in as part of your family office activities.

If you and your family already have defined your values, please jump directly to Step 6, unless you wish to revisit your values and co-create new, shared values.

Step 1

Each family member should go through the illustrated list of values and select their top five personal values. Feel free to add any additional values if they are not represented in the table. One way to do this is to use post-it notes and to write down one value per note. This will make it easy for you to move them around in later stages.

Step 2

Each family member should go through the list of values again and select the five values that they believe best characterize their family and which could form the basis for the family values moving forward. Compare the values you selected for yourself and for your family. Are they the same? Are they different? What does that signify?

List of values

☐ Achievement	☐ Faith	☐ Love
☐ Adaptability	☐ Forgiveness	☐ Loyalty
☐ Altruism	☐ Friendship	☐ Motivation
☐ Authenticity	☐ Frugality	☐ Openness
☐ Autonomy	☐ Fun	☐ Optimism
☐ Caring	☐ Generosity	☐ Passion
☐ Cohesion	☐ Gratitude	☐ Performance
☐ Compassion	☐ Happiness	☐ Recognition
☐ Competence	☐ Harmony	☐ Relationships
☐ Confidence	☐ Health	☐ Reliability
☐ Courage	☐ Honesty	☐ Reputation
☐ Creativity	☐ Humility	☐ Respect
☐ Curiosity	☐ Humor	☐ Responsibility
☐ Discipline	☐ Impact	☐ Social responsibility
☐ Diversity	☐ Independence	☐ Service
☐ Duty	☐ Inner peace	☐ Spirituality
☐ Empathy	☐ Innovativeness	☐ Stewardship
☐ Empowerment	☐ Integrity	☐ Success
☐ Engagement	☐ Kindness	☐ Tradition
☐ Entrepreneurialism	☐ Leadership	☐ Trust
☐ Equality	☐ Learning	☐ Unity
☐ Fairness	☐ Legacy	☐ Vision
		☐ Wisdom

Step 3

Share the five family values which you have each selected in Step 2. Collect these values together onto a single sheet or flipchart. This will provide you with a visual overview of the similarities and differences of opinions that exist.

Step 4

You should now have all the values from your family in front of you. Cluster them by theme or category. It is likely that some values will have been chosen by multiple family members. The more overlap you have, the easier this process becomes. There might also be values that are very similar: you might want to consider clustering these together and agreeing on a new / different terminology.

Step 5

If it isn't already clear what your top family values are from Step 4, deploy a voting system to agree on your top three to five values, with a list of "maybe" values as a backup.

Step 6

Start thinking about the meaning and implications of each of your values in the context of your family office. In this step, we will ask you to explain how each value could be translated into key decisions regarding the family office. To illustrate this, we have shared a few examples in the table below.

Value	What is the meaning / implication of this value for your (future) family office?
1	
2	
3	
e.g., Social responsibility	It is important that our spectrum of activities and investments takes into consideration the social responsibility of our family. This relates to our family-specific activities, our businesses and investment activities, as well as our impact investing and philanthropic activities. The role of the family office should be to ensure a holistic "doing good by doing well" philosophy.
e.g., Unity	We want to make sure that our family office supports individual family members and the wider family through activities and initiatives to foster family unity.
e.g., Loyalty	We value long-term relationships in our business as a family. Therefore, our family office should seek to identify and work with reliable partners over multiple years, if not generations.

ACTIVITY 4:
DESIGN YOUR "FAMILY MANIFESTO"

You have now mapped out your family enterprise ecosystem, your aspirational future for this ecosystem, and your family values. It's now time to put together your "family manifesto".

The family manifesto will serve as a solid base for the design (or redesign) of your family office. It gives you, your family, your family office employees and your ecosystem partners a clear sense of direction for where you wish to go and how the family office should help you get there.

An effective and meaningful family manifesto is, ultimately, a constellation of three key elements:

- Your family vision or purpose
- Your family "glue"
- Your family values

As a family, discuss the following questions to help you write your manifesto:

- Why, for what, and for whom do we want to stay together over the next 25 years?
- What keeps us united today and what will keep us together in the future?
- Why are we better off together than alone?
- What changes would we like to see in our own lives and in the world?
- How do we want to leverage our total family wealth for maximum impact?
- What legacy do we want to create for our children?
- What will be the state of our family in a perfect future world?
- How are we going to work with one another in the future?
- Will there be a strong sense of connection and family togetherness?

Our family vision / purpose statement
What is keeping us together today and in the future (our glue)?
Our family values (add from Activity 3)

CONCLUSION

Congratulations! You have successfully completed the first part of the *Navigator* project and laid the foundation for the design of your family office.

Status quo of our family enterprise ecosystem		Aspirations for the future of our family enterprise ecosystem
	OUR FAMILY MANIFESTO	

Equipped with this knowledge, we will next move on to the core of the *Family Office Navigator*, the "Family Office Strategy House," where we will first define the purpose of your family office, before identifying its focus and then designing its organizational structure.

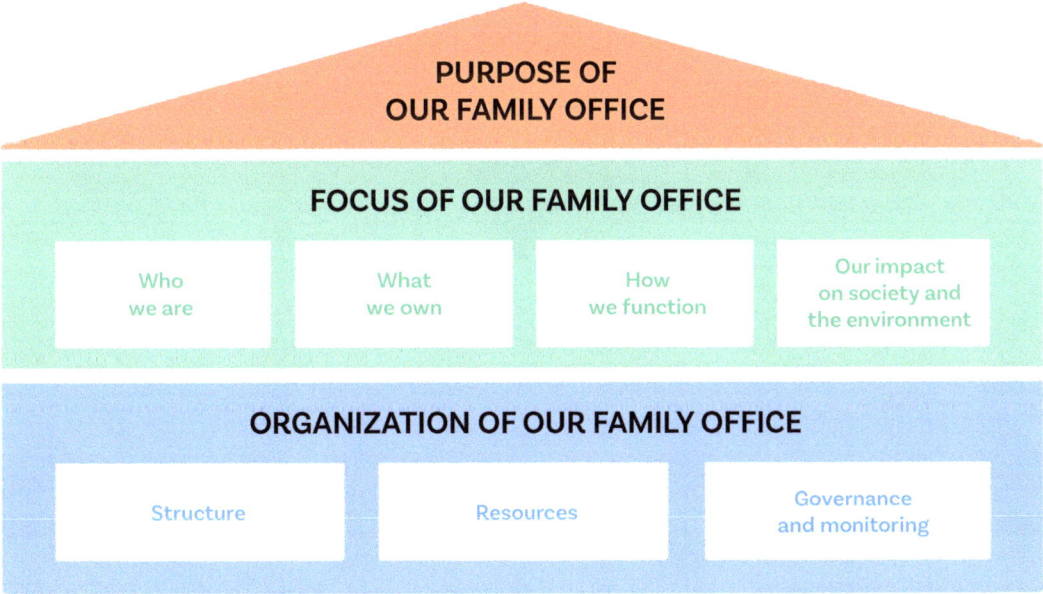

PURPOSE OF OUR FAMILY OFFICE

FOCUS OF OUR FAMILY OFFICE

Who we are	What we own	How we function	Our impact on society and the environment

ORGANIZATION OF OUR FAMILY OFFICE

Structure	Resources	Governance and monitoring

CHAPTER 3

PURPOSE OF YOUR FAMILY OFFICE

Define the purpose of your family office by protecting your family's legacy and shaping your future aspirations.

«Your purpose of life is to find your purpose and give your whole heart and soul to it.»

Siddhartha Gautama (Buddha)

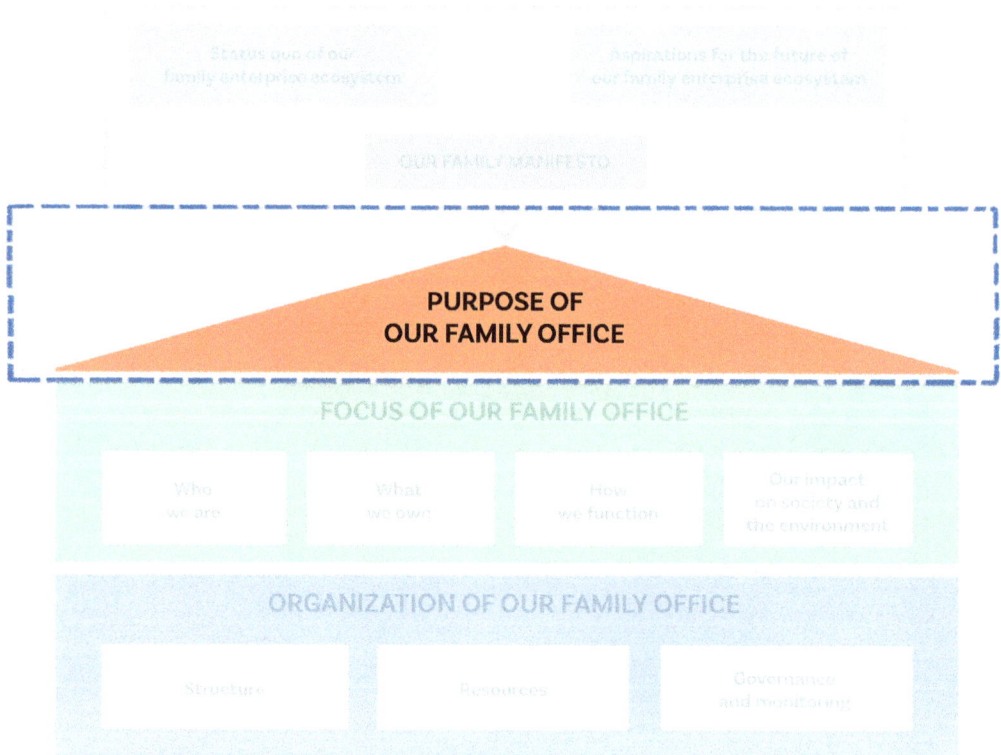

Welcome to the "Purpose" chapter of the *Family Office Navigator*. In the previous chapter, you had a chance to map your family enterprise ecosystem, your total family wealth, and your family manifesto. Hopefully, these exercises have helped you understand the various needs and complexities of your system.

You are getting closer to defining what your family office will do and look like, but before defining the specific services, setup, and governance of your (future) family office, we believe that it is important to discuss its purpose. We encourage you to take time in this chapter to explore and define your family office's purpose – why it exists or should exist.

In this chapter, you will:

- ☑ Reflect on why purpose matters for your family office (and family).
- ☑ Understand what a family office purpose statement is and why you should develop one.
- ☑ Consider the different choices at play that will inform your family office purpose statement, depending on where you are on your journey as a family.
- ☑ Explore examples of how other families at different stages of the journey approach and define the purpose of their family office.
- ☑ Work together as a family to explore options for your family office's purpose.
- ☑ As a family, craft a clear and concise family office purpose statement. Use your work from the last chapter, "Charting Your Course", to inform your purpose statement.
- ☑ Put your purpose statement to work, guiding you and your family through the next steps of the *Navigator* and the future path of your family office.

WHY PURPOSE MATTERS

It might be tempting to think that defining a purpose for your family office is unnecessary – perhaps a luxury, a waste of time, too esoteric and vague, or too hard. Nothing could be further from the truth. A purpose is a fundamental ingredient for your family office and family. In our ecological ecosystem analogy, it is the meaning of life. We would go so far as to say that without a purpose, a family office is missing fundamental meaning – its ultimate objective, its North Star, its direction. A family office without a clear purpose cannot have a coherent, cohesive and holistic focus, and risks failure from the start.

Whether your family is starting your family office because of a significant transition (e.g., a liquidity event or a generational transition) or you are rein-venting an existing family office to meet evolving circumstances, it is crucial to deliberately define your family office's purpose at this fork in the road.

With so much at stake – from your family's wealth and relationships to its future trajectory – this is not the time to cut corners and leapfrog this important step. After all, purpose is a key pillar of any professional, organizational, or personal undertaking. It provides direction, motivation, and meaning to what we do. Family offices without a clear purpose risk becoming a melting pot of activities that have no cohesion or strategy. Operationally, they become chaotic and reactive, rather than planful and intentional. This can lead to poor asset allocation decisions, poor hiring choices, inefficiencies, wasted resources, as well as possibly creating tension within the family.

In contrast, defining a purpose for your family office guides the role the office will have in the future, and establishes the foundations for a holistic and cohesive journey, in which all areas of activity, governance, and organization are aligned. In defining a purpose for your family office, you should consider your family's total wealth, your aspirations for the future and manifesto (your work from the prior chapter) to ensure that, whatever the family office does, it is fully aligned with your family's current and future needs and wishes.

Your family's legacy may have been built on the hard work and vision of one or two individuals who built a family business from scratch. Setting up or reshaping a family office is very much like starting a new entrepreneurial venture for your family. All successful entrepreneurial endeavours have one thing in common: a clearly defined, ambitious, and exciting purpose. In recent years, the importance of purpose has become mainstream as many large organizations seek to redraw their social contracts with employees, customers, suppliers and their wider ecosystem. You will want to do the same for your family office, approaching it with the same sense of gravity as any new venture that requires the family's capital and time.

A purpose statement for your family office

A clearly defined family office purpose fundamentally answers these overarching questions, from the vantage point of the family: Why does our family office exist? What are we trying to accomplish with our family office? What are we building together with this family office?

It is best articulated in a purpose statement. This written document serves as a record of what the family wants to achieve and formalizes what some families may be tempted to leave unspoken. We believe that writing down a family office purpose statement is critical because:

- It provides clarity on why the family office exists, what it is meant to achieve, and what the family office does and why. This serves as an important anchor and reference for family members and family office employees.
- It creates cohesion and alignment between family members with respect to what they want from their family office.
- It helps establish trust between different stakeholder groups.
- It provides guidance to family office executives on what the family office should achieve and do to ensure alignment with the family's intentions for the office.

It may be that you and your family already have a formalized family vision, mission, purpose, or manifesto. That's a great starting point from which you can derive the purpose of your family office. The purpose of your family office should support the family's greater purpose. If managed and positioned well, the family office can become a platform that helps you fulfill your individual mission and your family's collective mission as a family of wealth in the world.

A lack of alignment between the purpose of the family and the purpose and role of the family office can lead to major conflicts - amongst the family, but also with the family office staff. Ultimately, you want to ensure that everyone is on the same page and that the activities of the family office are in service of its purpose.

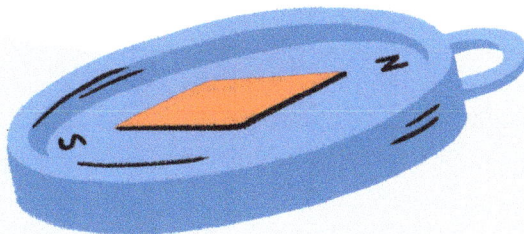

Life changes, and so does purpose

Your family enterprise ecosystem is continuously changing. Circumstances change, your family is evolving and changing (in size and complexity), your business activities and investments develop, the roles of different members of the family ebb and flow, new views and ways emerge, and your external environment (economic and political) is in a state of constant flux. As your family enterprise ecosystem transforms over time, it is only natural that the role of your family office will need to adapt, or risk becoming inefficient or irrelevant. This means that the purpose statement of your family office will need to be reviewed at various stages of the journey to ensure it remains relevant as the North Star of your family office. After all, your statement might have been written by relatives who no longer need its services. We recommend that you review your purpose statement with your family, and following the steps in this chapter, at sensible medium-term intervals or whenever a significant transition occurs, such as a liquidity event or a transfer of control across generations.

STRATEGIC CHOICES

There are many factors that influence the process of defining the purpose of your family office. These can include, for example, where you are as a family and where you want to go, triggering events that have brought you to this point, the nature and complexity of your family enterprise ecosystem, the timeframe that you have in mind (short- to mid-term or multi-generational) and the needs and priorities of your family.

Because of these multiple influences, there is no boilerplate family office purpose statement that can be offered to you, nor do we recommend you seek one to copy, paste, and adopt. It is a worthy exercise to dialogue with your family – as many times as needed – about what you each truly want your family office to be and achieve, and work through your differences to arrive at a unified purpose you can support. Your family office purpose should be uniquely yours.

Create an inclusive process

While our experience shows that defining a purpose for your family office brings benefits and not doing so creates challenges and risks, there is another compelling reason to agree on a purpose statement. We have seen the positive impact that the process of discussing and creating a purpose statement has on families: the journey is just as important as the destination.

We often see that one or a few family members take the lead with respect to the initiation of the family office. That is a natural and pragmatic approach. It is typical that the wider family puts trust in one individual or a representative group of individuals to work on this assignment. However, the risk of fully delegating these foundational steps to an individual or small group - without the family contributing - is that the family becomes disconnected and disengaged from the family office. If you find yourselves saying, "*He / She is the most qualified, so let us have him / her work out the details and set things up for us,*" proceed with caution, because you are entering problematic territory. From our experience working with families and their family offices, and having studied many more family offices, we know that this can lead to disengagement of family members and even misalignment and major conflicts between family members. Take the example of a failed investment that the individual or small group agreed to make on behalf of the family, without the family having had a chance to reflect on or express their expectations. Family conflict is almost inevitable. This can be avoided with an inclusive process.

Engaging the wider family members to exchange and share views on the purpose of your family office fosters greater buy-in, alignment and understanding – in effect, acting as a communication space for the family to forge a path forward that unites them.

However, while you want to make sure to invite everybody from the family to participate in these discussions to capture the different prevailing perspectives, needs and wishes, it is important to not stifle the process by making it too cumbersome or requiring unanimous agreement. It makes sense to have an effective decision-making process and body (e.g., a sub-committee of interested and capable family members) that is mandated by the family to take the lead. This group should then be mandated to collect the views of other family members, where needed, and to provide an update to the entire family or branch representatives.

We have identified five strategic choices that we believe are critical for you and your family to review and discuss as you embark on defining the purpose of your (future) family office.

We advise you to take each of these choices in turn and discuss the options with your family, so that you can come to a consensus on your joint views. This process will allow you to gain clarity and should make it a lot easier for you to formulate the purpose statement of your family office.

There is no right answer to any of these strategic choices, and different family members are likely to have diverse views. This is natural in a family. It is wise to work collaboratively, to collect and consider all opinions, to treat family members' views as legitimate, and then to develop viable options that will work for the collective. The process of exploring each choice and opinion is as important as the outcome – it helps develop respect and trust within the family as well as a shared understanding about what the future should look like and how a family office can help.

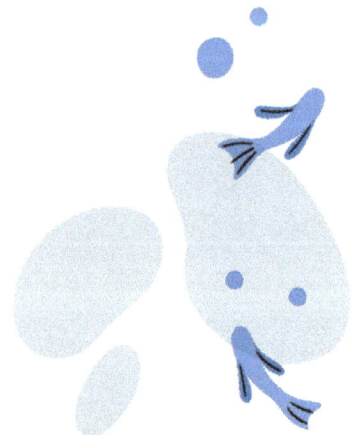

1. *Ask yourself*: Do we want our family office to meet …

IMMEDIATE NEEDS		LONG-TERM NEEDS

Short- to mid-term priorities of the family

Are you primarily concerned with immediate / short-term needs that you have (e.g., putting together an investment strategy for money you and the family have received through a liquidity event) or are you trying to set up a structure that builds the foundation for multi-generational unity and success? It is likely that, especially over time, there will be a mix of short-, mid-, and long-term needs, although some may not be as important as others at this very moment. These needs are constantly evolving. Understanding these elements and their relative importance to you and your family will help you to align the family and serve as an important basis for defining the purpose of your family office. It also serves as useful guidance to any family officers who are working with and for the family.

Long-term, multi-generational priorities of the family

2. *Ask yourself*: Do we want our family office to focus on …

PRESERVING LEGACY		DRIVING RENEWAL

Preserving and transferring family traditions, values, legacy business activities and assets

As we discussed earlier in the book, there are different reasons why families wish to set up a family office. One important factor to consider is whether the primary purpose is to preserve legacy and to protect / transfer existing aspects of the family enterprise ecosystem across generations or whether the primary purpose is to create the foundation for something new (e.g., because the legacy family business has been sold and the family wishes to redefine itself, seeking out a new identity and purpose). Sometimes it is a combination of both.

Changing direction and / or starting a new journey through novel or different business / investment activities

3. Ask yourself: Do we want our family office to primarily manage ...

FINANCIAL CAPITAL – HUMAN CAPITAL – SOCIAL CAPITAL

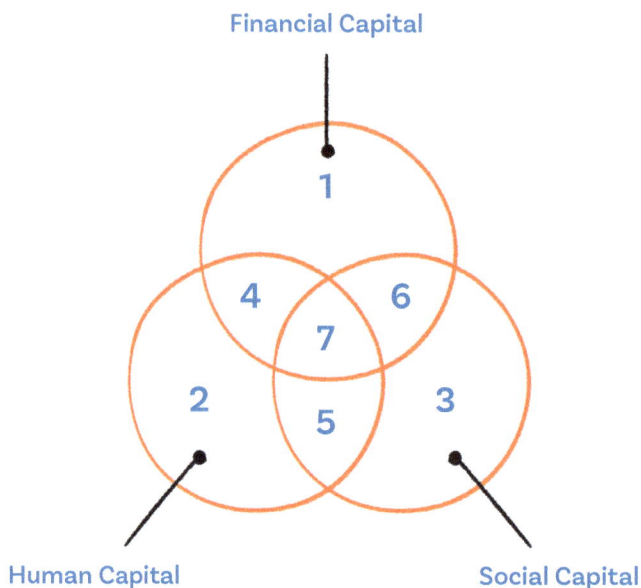

As you embark on or reassess your family office journey, it is useful to reflect on where you want the emphasis of the family office to lie; whether the exclusive goal is to manage the financial capital (#1 in the diagram), a mix of financial capital and human capital (#4 in the diagram) or any other combination.

While we will delve deeper into the specific focus areas and services for your family office in the next chapter, it is useful to reflect at a high-level at this point, taking into consideration the assessment you made of the status quo of your family enterprise ecosystem in the previous chapter. Depending on where you see complexities in the system – who we are, what we own, how we function, our role in society – your primary motivation and focus will be different. This will depend on the stage of evolution that you and your family enterprise ecosystem are in.

As we elaborated on in the previous chapter, most family offices are initially established because the family wishes to manage their financial assets, whether from a liquidity event or accumulation outside the legacy business (e.g., portfolio of investments or real estate). However, it is not uncommon that there is a combination of several factors and, most important, that this will change and evolve over time.

4. *Ask yourself*: Who do we want the family office to serve ...

Who will be the primary (or at least initial) customer of your family office? Is it just you? Is it your branch? Is it your larger family? Would you consider making it accessible to other families that you know well or even to other families of wealth that you are not familiar with? These are important strategic choices you should make as they lay out the terms for your family office's purpose as well as many organizational aspects. Evidently, if you intend to serve multiple families, then the scale and infrastructure you need will be quite different than if you intend to have a family office for your own personal needs.

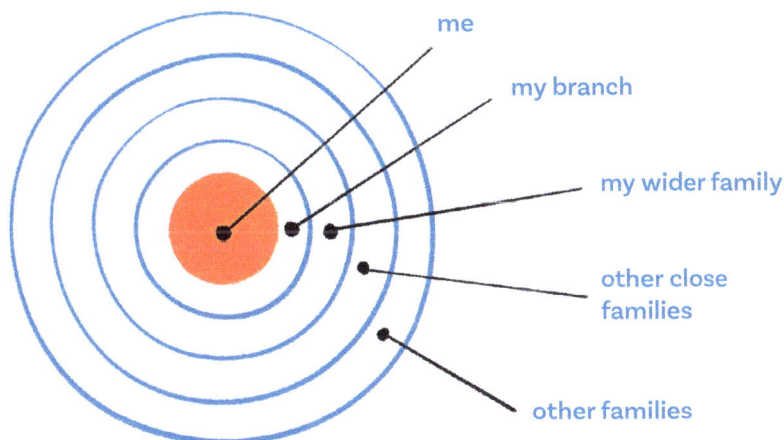

me

my branch

my wider family

other close families

other families

5. *Ask yourself*: Do I, or do we, need a dedicated family office, or could our needs be served by an existing multi-family office or by creating a hybrid family office structure?

At this stage, it might be useful to revisit the various types of family offices we introduced in the "Introduction" chapter. We will revisit these and discuss different structural choices in the "Organizing your Family Office" chapter, providing you with some guidance as to whether a single family office makes sense for you and your family or if you are better served with an alternative setup.

Now that we have looked at the different strategic choices that will shape and inform the fundamentals of your purpose statement, it is time to look at the way other families, at various stages of maturity, shape their own family office purpose. You will have a chance to return to and systematically work through these strategic choices in Activity 2 at the end of this chapter.

LEARN FROM YOUR PEERS

"If you have seen one family office, you have seen one family office."

A quote frequently used in the family offices community

This statement is widely used in the field to illustrate that no two family offices are alike and that, therefore, it is of critical importance that you focus on your own family's wishes and needs when designing your family office. This approach makes sense because no two family enterprise ecosystems are alike. Your ecosystem is truly unique and, consequently, the needs you have for a family office are different from any other family.

Nonetheless, our research has shown that there are certain patterns and identities of family offices. Those that faced similar goals and challenges to you can act as frames of reference to help you design your own family office journey. In the previous chapter, we introduced different archetypes of family enterprise ecosystems, including the founder / controlling owner archetype, the evolving / maturing family business archetype, and the large / dynastic family archetype. We believe it can be helpful to explore how families that fall into these archetypal categories have shaped their purpose statements for their family offices at different stages of the journey.

The following examples should provide some helpful, thought-provoking, and inspiring ideas to enrich your own reflections and discussions as a family. Remember that we do not recommend you copy, paste and adopt any of these examples.

Let's look at how each family approached the concept of purpose as part of designing or finetuning their family office. Here are a few examples of family office purpose statements as they can be found on the websites of the respective family offices. We deliberately chose to showcase only publicly visible purpose statements at this stage.

Examples of family office purpose statements

Example 1: Anthos (family office of the Brenninkmeijer family)

Anthos is the family office dedicated to advancing the success of the owners' endeavours and the flourishing of the Brenninkmeijer family community. Anthos helps the owners of COFRA past and present focus on their business and philanthropic activities, offering support to their families.

Example 2: JAB Holding (investment office of the Reimann family)

JAB invests in consumer goods and services and is focused on long-term value creation through its unique platform investing philosophy.

Example 3: Korys (investment office of the Colruyt family)

Korys is the investment company of the Colruyt family. We manage the estate of the Colruyt family, championing value-driven business practices by investing in people and companies. We believe an attractive return is perfectly compatible with a positive contribution to people, the environment and society.

A few other, anonymous, examples include:

- Driven by the desire to create a healthy, fair, and equitable world for the future, we invest in the future of food and water.
- Our mission is to steward our legacy, cultivating growth through strategic investments while upholding our commitment to societal betterment and sustainable practices.
- Building on our entrepreneurial spirit, we pursue investments that drive innovation, foster business growth, and generate long-term value.Our family's commitment to a sustainable future guides our investments, emphasizing both financial return and positive environmental impact.

NOTE: These are rather short and crisp statements for the public eye. Evidently, not all family offices will have such a public profile and if they do then the family might choose to have a longer, more elaborate purpose statement for internal purposes. This is up to you and your family to choose.

As you can see from the examples, purpose statements look very different from one family office to the next. However, as a guiding rule, it is important for an effective family office purpose statement to follow these design principles:

- ☑ It should be uniquely yours and not simply a copy-paste from another family office.
- ☑ It should express your aspirations, describing not only the status quo of what the family office focuses on, but also providing guidance for future direction.
- ☑ It should be clear about what the family wishes to achieve in the world with the family office's support.
- ☑ It should neither be too narrow or technical, nor too broad and unspecific.
- ☑ It should truly reflect the family's identity and values and the way the family wishes to be perceived in the world.

ACTIVITIES

Now that you have explored your options for the most important strategic choices that will influence the purpose of your family office and looked at how other families approach the question of purpose, we will lead you through some structured exercises that will bring all these insights together to help you draft your own family office purpose statement.

This process will also draw on the outcome of your family discussions during the "Charting Your Course" chapter – information that will serve as a guiding light for your journey throughout the *Family Office Navigator*.

As in the previous chapter, we recommend that you convene the key members of your family for these activities, taking the necessary time away from your busy lives and distractions to ensure that you make the most of the process – both in terms of defining the most appropriate purpose statement for your family office, but also to grow in understanding of each other as a family. It may be wise to engage a professional facilitator with experience in family workshops to help improve the management, impact and outcome of your reflections.

> **Family Office Navigator questions:**
>
> · How will our family office help us manage the present and prepare for the future of our family enterprise ecosystem?

ACTIVITY 1:
TRIGGERING EVENTS FOR SETTING UP A FAMILY OFFICE

In the "Introduction" chapter, we spoke about the different triggering events that lead families to consider setting up a family office. At this stage, we advise that you and your family revisit and go through this list and select all the different triggering events that you, individually and then collectively, consider relevant for you.

Step 1

Individually, go through the (non-exhaustive) list of possible triggering events below and select those which you think apply to you and your family. We have also added a "wild card" in case there is another reason that you can think of which has not been listed. If you choose this wild card, ensure that you define and communicate the additional reason / triggering event.

Step 2

Gather all family members and present your selections to each other. It might be advisable to record your choices on a flipchart or a sheet of paper, highlighting possible overlaps as well as possible differences.

Step 3

Engage in an open discussion around the areas where you overlap as a family and the areas where you have different points of view. Aligning on the reason(s) for why you wish to set up a family office, as well as recognizing any divergence, is an important step as you prepare the ground for the formulation of your family office purpose statement.

- Liquidity events (partial or total sale of business, dividends ...)
- Desire for control and more independence (e.g., from banks, accountants, ...)
- Achieve excellence in investment management
- Support family & ownership governance & act as nexus to business
- Create a hub for the family (to foster unity, develop talents, ...)
- Wish for personalization/customization
- Desire to delegate burden of wealth management
- Protect family privacy, anonymity and confidentiality
- Preserve family wealth & support inter-generational wealth management
- Consolidated reporting and centralized risk management
- Gain access to unconventional investment opportunities
- Active deal sourcing and pipeline management
- Status

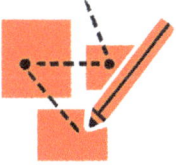

ACTIVITY 2:
MAKING SENSE OF YOUR STRATEGIC CHOICES

In this activity, we will examine the strategic decisions that you explored earlier in this chapter and help you harness that information in the context of the purpose of your family office. How do your strategic choices influence and shape your collective purpose statement?

Gather your family to review the answers and decisions you came to, while reviewing each of the strategic choices presented in this chapter:

1. Immediate needs vs. Long-term needs
2. Preserving legacy vs. Driving renewal
3. Primary motivation is the management of Financial capital – Human capital – Social capital
4. Family office customer(s)
5. Type of family office

Step 1

Individually, go through the five strategic choices and reflect on your point of view on each of them. The following questions might help you in this reflection process:

- Which strategic choices are more relevant or important for you than others?
- What are your reasons for choosing one way or another?

Step 2

Gather as a family and present your perspectives on each of these strategic choices.

- Where is the common ground for each choice?
- What are the differences of opinion for each choice?
- Can you see a narrative or shared perspective forming around your answers?

Compare notes and, ideally, agree on a shared position for each strategic choice. If there is too much dissonance or it is difficult to agree, it may be worth considering how to reflect that in your purpose statement.
Does the family office need to cater to different needs, perspectives, groups and / or individuals? Could there be some structural choices that you can make to accommodate the different wishes and needs of individuals within the family (e.g., a hybrid family office setup, a model we will be discussing later).

Step 3

Once you have agreed on a list of priorities for your purpose statement and a position for each strategic choice, try to condense that information into a few paragraphs. These paragraphs will form the foundation for the next exercise.

ACTIVITY 3:
FROM AN INDIVIDUAL TO A COLLECTIVE VIEW

In this activity, we will embrace the diversity of views in your family to spark a meaningful discussion about the priorities for your purpose statement. This will help you move towards and then agree on a unified statement that will provide a sound foundation for the next steps in the *Navigator* and the life of your family office.

Step 1

Split up into small groups or individuals, depending on the dynamics of your family, and take some time to sketch out how you would like to frame the purpose statement for your family office. Consider starting by completing this prompt: *Our family office exists to …*

Bear in mind all the information and insights you have generated from the start of this book to this point and reflect on your own personal needs, outlook, and ambitions. In the "Charting Your Course" chapter you should have developed your family manifesto. Make sure you have this to hand at this stage of your journey as a basis for the discussion.

By the end of this step, each small group or individual should have completed a succinct but comprehensive statement that sums up how they see the purpose of the family office.

Step 2

It is now time to come together to share your purpose statements. First, write them all down together in a way that they are visible to the full group, then give each individual or small group an opportunity to read out their statement and then explain the thinking behind the wording.

Step 3

You will need to appoint a note-taker for this step. Discuss and review the strengths, weaknesses, similarities and differences of each proposal and jot down or map out the outcomes of these reflections. You will soon start to find common ground around the core elements that are important for everyone and begin working out which factors are less relevant for the group.

One approach that might be helpful to visualize similarities and differences here could be to highlight specific keywords that each person or group used in their drafts and try to map those words out across the wider group. It is also important to ask: Are any keywords missing? Are your statements aligned with your family manifesto?

Step 4

Drawing on the results of the previous steps, work on drafting a family office purpose statement which reflects the group's perspective and consensus. This may take longer than you think, but it will be worth it now and in the future. It is advisable to do this in an iterative way, reviewing and revising the wording until it hits the mark.

TIME PUT TO GOOD PURPOSE

The first step in the *Family Office Navigator* is complete. You have developed a high-level perspective of the purpose of your family office and crafted, with your family, a purpose statement that reflects your agreed-upon, shared position on why your family office exists and what it is aiming to achieve. You've integrated the reflections and outcomes from the "Charting Your Course" chapter and the activities in this chapter. You are making great progress!

This is a defining moment for your (future) family office and positions you strongly for the next steps of the *Navigator* and the future success of your family office. Many families avoid having these conversations because they are afraid of the conflicts that might arise during the discussion and because they lack a structured, guided approach. However, despite the struggles you may have faced while trying to agree on a shared purpose for your family office, it will serve you and the family well and, hopefully, will prevent tensions and challenges further down the road. We hope that these efforts will underpin, inform and enhance your journey.

As we have mentioned, do not be afraid to revisit your purpose statement when it feels right to do so. Your purpose, like your family and its family office, is an evolving feature in your ever-changing, dynamic ecosystem.

The next step in the *Navigator* is to define the focus of your family office – the specific services that you require to meet your current needs and to set you on the right course to achieve your future goals as a family.

So, let's get focused!

CHAPTER 4

FOCUS OF YOUR FAMILY OFFICE

Define the core activities and services of your family office to help you manage your total family wealth and your family enterprise ecosystem.

"Focus is about making choices and deciding what you are NOT going to do."

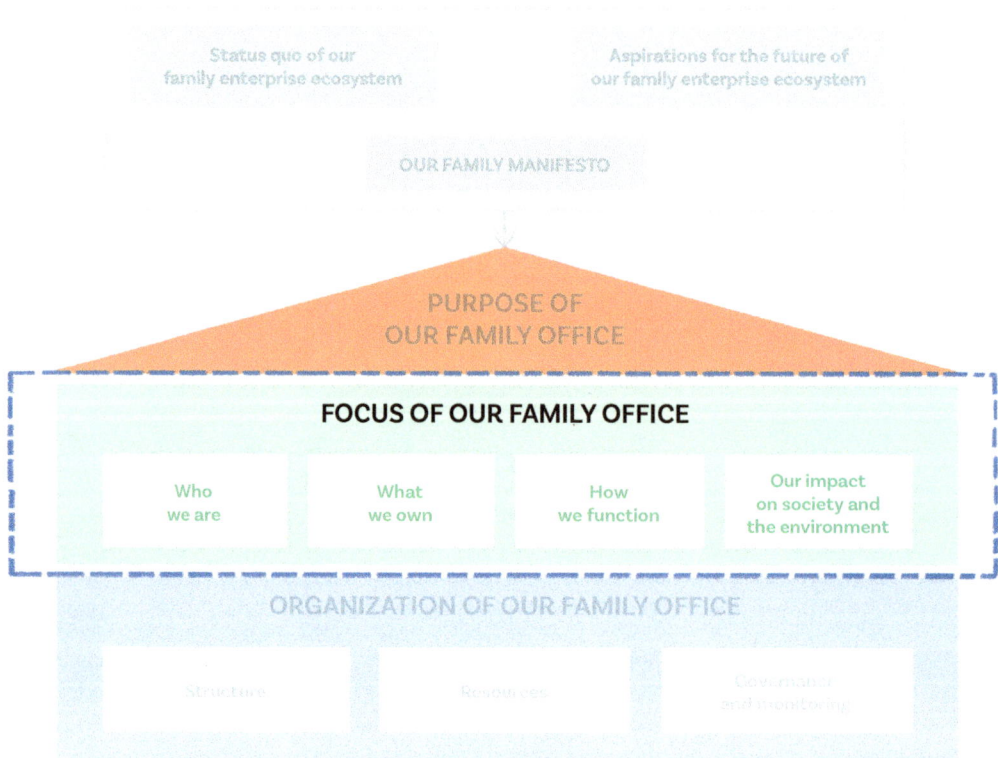

Status quo of our
family enterprise ecosystem

Aspirations for the future of
our family enterprise ecosystem

OUR FAMILY MANIFESTO

PURPOSE OF
OUR FAMILY OFFICE

FOCUS OF OUR FAMILY OFFICE

| Who we are | What we own | How we function | Our impact on society and the environment |

ORGANIZATION OF OUR FAMILY OFFICE

| Structure | Resources | Governance and monitoring |

By this stage in your journey, you have developed a clear understanding of your present and future family enterprise ecosystem, drafted your family manifesto and defined the purpose of your family office. In this chapter, we will discuss the focus of your family office.

When we talk about the focus of a family office, we are referring to the type and scope of services as well as the support that the family office will provide for you and your family. For example:

- What will your family office do for you on a day-to-day, year-by-year, individual or collective basis?
- What areas of services and responsibilities will it address for your family?
- Will it be exclusively focused on financial matters, or will it also provide a variety of other non-financial services and support activities?
- Will it have a strategic role, integrated into the overall family enterprise system, or will it stand somewhat separate from your other business activities?
- Will it be short-, medium- or long-term oriented?
- Which services will be run in-house and which will be outsourced?
- Who in the family will it serve?
- Will it be simple or complex?

In this chapter, you will make decisions about what the roles and responsibilities of your family office will be.

Think about your options for creating a family office on a spectrum of possibilities. On one end, a family office with the most narrow scope is an informal vehicle for managing financial matters, such as investing the proceeds of a liquidity event. On the other end of the spectrum, the family office, wide in scope, is a robust, holistic platform structured to offer many services that preserve and nurture the family's total wealth, perhaps starting with investing but branching out into other financial areas such as real estate, legal and tax matters, and insurance; then expanding out further into family talent development, fostering family cohesion, overseeing the family's overarching asset allocation towards impact and philanthropy, concierge services such as travel or home maintenance and even personal health and well-being.

Wherever you land on the spectrum, whichever path you take, and whatever stage of the journey you are at, the services and functions of the family office should be considered, selected, and designed deliberately and collectively with the long-term wellbeing of the family enterprise system in mind. No matter how humble or elaborate your ambitions for your family office are, it is vital to set aside time as a family to explore the diverse options and possibilities that a family office can offer before deciding what to include or exclude from yours. Engage in a collaborative, exploratory process with your family. Listen to each other and understand the different needs of family members. This will help you design your family office, prepare for the future evolution of the family office, and avoid conflicts or misunderstandings.

It is inevitable that the individual and group needs of the family in relation to its family office will evolve and shift over time. The focus of your family office will adjust accordingly. In the founding stage, it makes sense to start small with a specific focus. At a later stage, with more generations in the family, or as circumstances change, your family office will need to evolve and perhaps develop a more holistic set of services.

From simple to sophisticated.

An example of the evolution of the family office focus over time, names changed for confidentiality reasons

Background:

- 2nd generation family business with 60 years of history
- Family: Steve (founder, retired), his children Paula and Mike (G2). Paula is the CEO of the business. Mike sits on the board but is not operationally involved.
- Paula and Mike co-owned the business (each holding 50% of the shares).
- Until recently, 95% of the family's wealth was bound in the legacy business, posing certain financial risks due to wealth concentration and exposure to a rather volatile market.
- The family went through a liquidity event (sale of 40% of the business to another family they know well).
- Paula and Mike organize themselves separately with respect to their liquid wealth obtained from the sale.

Phase 1: From liquidity to a classical investment office

- Paula and her husband David set up their own family office, with the primary focus of managing their branch's financials and to diversify.
- The model is a classical investment office.
- David manages the family office alongside two full-time, non-family investment professionals, with full focus on financial matters.
- This setup continues for several years, until the four members of the third generation reach their teenage years.

Phase 2: Serving G2 and G3

- The family office expands its activities to meet some of G3's needs.

- The goal is initially to educate and onboard G3, with a specific focus on responsible ownership, investments, impact investing and philanthropy.
- Later, the family office starts to expand its activities to serve the family's events and social activities.

Phase 3: Integration of the wider system's governance bodies

- Paula and David's family office has now become the primary "glue" of this branch of the family. The family now consists of the two parents (G2), the four children (G3) and their spouses as well as the 14 grandchildren (G4).
- The family system has become more complex, requiring more services on the human and social capital side. The financial activities have also evolved with more diversified activities.
- At this point, the legacy business "only" constitutes 20% of the family branch's total financial wealth. The family office acts as the holding company that is structured into different verticals, including the legacy business and a variety of strategic / growth investments as well as other initiatives and philanthropic endeavors.

In this chapter, we will describe the main service areas that family offices can offer. We will provide you with a clear framework to demystify the complex technical services available. We do so to help you understand how and where those services fit within your family's context, the important role they can play in building a holistic and cohesive ecosystem, and what is at stake for your family if you don't choose the optimal focus for your family office. We will do this without going into too many technical, financial details, as this would go beyond the scope of this book. However, if you are interested in delving deeper into more technical aspects, we recommend discussing them with a family office expert or financial professional.

Upon completing this chapter, you will have:

- ✔ Understood the main focus areas of family offices and their significance within your family enterprise ecosystem
- ✔ Learned about the spectrum of specific services available within these main focus areas
- ✔ Gained further clarity on your family's total wealth, including how your financial, social, and human capital interconnect and influence your present and future
- ✔ Explored the strategic choices that will shape your family office today and how they might evolve over time
- ✔ Learned techniques to come together as a family to reflect on and engage in structured conversations to help you decide on the focus of your family office for this current stage in your journey

WHAT CAN A FAMILY OFFICE DO FOR YOU?

While many families regard the family office primarily as a vehicle for financial investment, in this chapter, we encourage you to go beyond and explore how a family office can help you shape the future of your family ecosystem and contribute to its long-term health and success.

We have already outlined the areas of your family's total wealth that a family office can support and underscored the fact that this stretches well beyond finance into areas such as human and social capital. You may decide, after deeper reflection, that your family office should only have a narrow focus or informal structure, which could be the most appropriate choice at this moment, but the initial, broader exploration of this chapter will highlight options available for the future, as your family's needs evolve.

Many family businesses fail after a few generations because they do not adopt a holistic, long-term perspective when it comes to governance, wealth planning, generational transitions, and entrepreneurial renewal. The same can be said of the family office. While it is possible for a family office to provide just financial services to a family for many years, its greatest value comes from taking a more holistic and integrative view that positions the family office as a pivotal vehicle for the future direction of the family.

Based on our experience working with multi-generational families from around the world, we would argue that a more holistic approach towards the health and well-being of the family enterprise ecosystem is essential. As a flexible and agile platform, the family office can provide the means to do this, and much more.

To help you appreciate and understand the scope of services the family office can provide and the role that a family office can play in your journey, we will follow the logic of the four pillars outlined in the "Charting Your Course" chapter, where you mapped your family enterprise ecosystem.

The following table provides a list of typical family office services that fall into each of these four pillars. This will provide some structure for your reflections about which services are important to you and your family. As you go through this table, we recommend that you return and refer to your reflections from the "Charting Your Course" chapter, including your needs and complexities. Ideally, your family office services should mirror your specific needs.

Potential focus areas for family office services

The four pillars of family office services	Who are we as a family?	What do we own?	How do we function?	What is our role in society and our impact on the environment?
Family office orientation	*Family office services that help family members individually flourish and that help us remain an informed, united and harmonious family*	*Family office services that help us manage assets, liabilities, and cash flow within our family enterprise ecosystem*	*Family office services that help us ensure effective and cohesive governance and decision-making across all aspects of our family enterprise ecosystem*	*Family office services that help us ensure that we have the most positive impact on society and the environment*
Specific focus areas for the family office	**Human Capital:** • Education of family members broadly (e.g., funding for school) • Develop family members to capably serve the family enterprise (e.g., owner preparation, board member preparation) • Help family members in their professional development (e.g., leadership development, career building) • Ensure physical & psychological health (e.g., insurance, special treatments, support in difficult times) **Social Capital:** • Support the family in building a shared vision and a shared sense of identity • Foster good relationships, unity and trust across the family • Support the family community (family meetings, events, communication, etc.) • Provide family concierge services • Act as a sounding board regarding family issues and solutions	**Financial Capital:** • Execute the owners' investment strategy and policies • Ensure sufficient diversification of assets according to the investment policy • Help the family manage risk exposure • Manage the portfolio of assets, including businesses, investments, properties and other high-value assets (e.g., art, yachts, aircraft, collectibles) • Manage liquidity needs (for family and business entities) • Oversee budgeting & cash flow of the family • Handle liability management • Approve and execute transactions • Manage accounting and bill paying for the family • Provide tax planning and compliance for the family • Conduct wealth transfer planning • Offer regular, consolidated reporting for the family	• Support the family in ensuring effective and efficient governance for the family, ownership, business and investments • Support the family in continuity and succession matters • Manage the legal and tax matters of the family • Provide trusteeship services • House and archive various documents (e.g., history, ownership, legal, tax, compliance) • Perform administrative tasks for the family enterprise ecosystem (e.g., bookkeeping, mail, IT, office management) • Facilitate effective and transparent, two-way communication between the family and the enterprise	• Support the family with executing their philanthropic and overall social impact activities • Help the family develop a cohesive strategy across all the businesses, investing and philanthropic activities to maximize ESG impact (typically at the direction of the owners' council or family council) • Help the family in their personal sustainability initiatives and attendant lifestyle transitions • Help the family preserve and nurture its reputational capital through its impact activities

Who are we as a family?

The first pillar of the focus of the family office caters to the family's human and social capital. By that we mean the people and relationships that define your family and its ecosystem. In short, this is who you are as a family. Through this pillar, we see the family office as a platform to help each member of your family reach their potential while safeguarding the ecosystem as a whole and creating the right conditions for it to thrive.

Human capital

Human capital is one of the most valuable treasures of any family. If families want to succeed in the long-term, it is vital that family members follow a path of learning and development. For the next generation, this involves understanding who they are and where their interests and talents lie, and then developing the skills, tools and confidence which will allow them to be effective contributors and responsible owners within the family enterprise ecosystem. Many established family offices help families nurture family talents through education and coaching. Some family offices bring in outside advisors and specialists to help family members build the competencies that will allow them to be effective long-term owners and leaders of their family enterprise and wealth.

The family office's purview could also include fostering professional and academic development so that family members can fulfill certain professional roles and / or build the experience and attain the qualifications to help take crucial decisions in their own lives—whether inside or outside the family enterprise ecosystem. For example, helping family members learn how to be a good board member for the family business or helping family members develop as leaders in the community where they represent the family. At the same time, it could include services focusing on physical and mental health, covering topics such as insurance, access to clinics and treatments, and other more specific support mechanisms when required.

- **Education, development, and support of family members:** Ensuring that family members have a solid education helps to safeguard the long-term success of the wider family enterprise ecosystem. There are many ways in which family members can contribute to the health of their family enterprise ecosystem and it is important that families take a holistic view when it comes to preparing the next generation for potential roles. This can range from business activities to investments, philanthropy and entrepreneurial ventures. The next generation can contribute through governance roles as well as by taking on responsibilities relating to family matters, ownership and business operations. They can also act as social impact leaders for the family. And, of course, a vital and oftentimes undervalued role is raising the next generation of responsible owners.

What should be my role?

Family enterprise ecosystems offer a wide variety of potential roles for family members

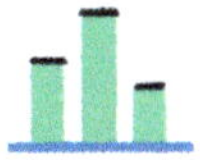

Business Employees

Leaders or managers in operating companies and other family corporations

Responsible Owners & Beneficiaries

of the family assets

Family Office Liaison

Coordinating with managers and strategic leaders in the Family Office

Governance Coordinators

Members and leaders of the Board of Directors, Family Council, etc.

Wealth Creators

Intrapreneur
Entrepreneur
Portfolio builder

Family Leaders

Working on the family's overall strategy & direction

Managing change, conflict and fairness

Social Impact Leaders

Managers and strategic leaders of family social impact activities

Healthy Adults

Good members of the family

Good parents of the NxG

Family offices can play a crucial role in two ways: by actively educating family members on topics which are important for wealth owners and by providing guidance, support, and even financial assistance when it comes to access to schools or universities. Family offices can also serve as a "go-to" hub for individuals who seek advice and mentoring for their personal career development, or when they are in a moment of reflection or personal crisis and need some guidance and structure.

Learning and development programs

An example of a structured educational offering whereby the family office plays a central organizational role in putting together and managing different programs and activities for the different age groups

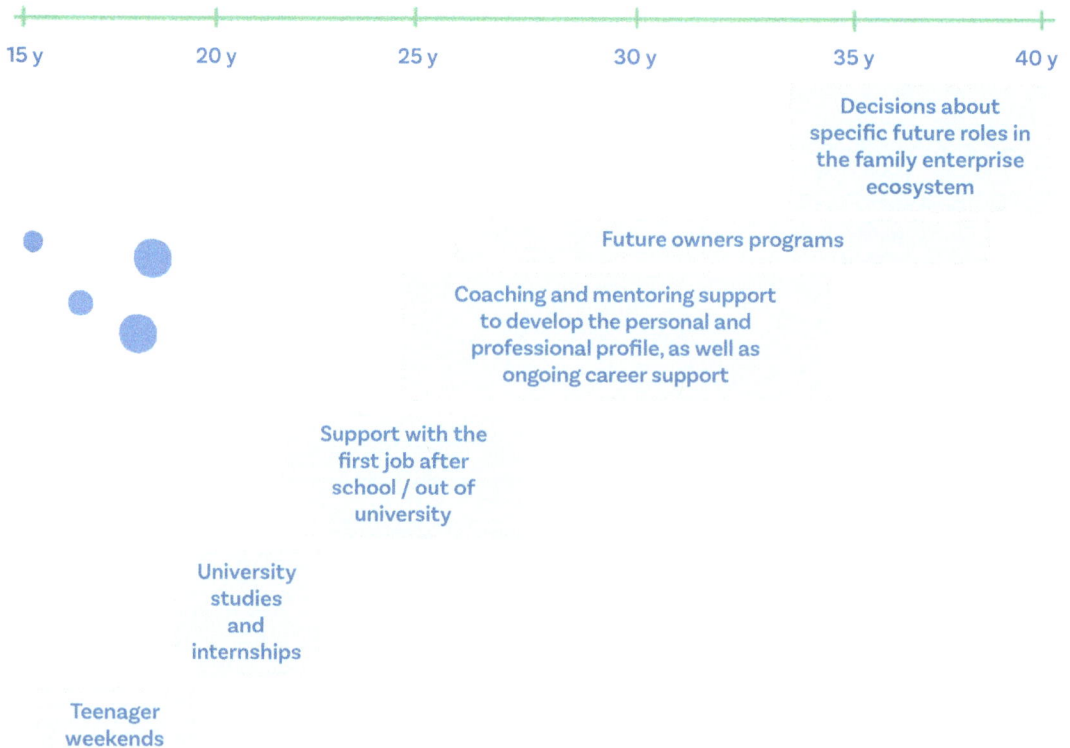

15 y	20 y	25 y	30 y	35 y	40 y

Decisions about specific future roles in the family enterprise ecosystem

Future owners programs

Coaching and mentoring support to develop the personal and professional profile, as well as ongoing career support

Support with the first job after school / out of university

University studies and internships

Teenager weekends

- **Physical and mental health:** Health and wellbeing for our loved ones and ourselves is the foundation for all things. As long as we are healthy, we might not actively think about who the best doctors might be or proactively plan for check-ups. Yet when there is a sudden illness, things sometimes need to happen very quickly. Navigating the complex medical and psychiatric system, finding the right clinics, doctors, or services can be difficult and time-consuming, especially in times of stress. Also, the coordination across different health-related platforms and systems can be complex. A family office can provide the necessary structure and guidance - discreetly – for organizing health-related matters in the background. Large, multi-generational families typically encompass a broad spectrum of individual wealth, with some individuals having greater wealth and others being less affluent. Yet, it might be the wish of the family that everybody has access to good healthcare, irrespective of their individual financial situation. In that sense, the family office can serve as a unique platform for the wider family.

Social capital

Beyond the human needs of a healthy, balanced family, we also include social capital, the value that derives from strong relationships and networks within the family ecosystem. For example, building a long-term future requires the development of a shared vision and sense of identity. Enhancing social capital also means nurturing strong and cooperative relationships within the family to foster unity. Structures can be put in place, managed by the family office, to support these goals through family community events, open discussions, knowledge sharing and other forms of communication. The family office can also become a platform that supports the family through concierge services that take the strain off individuals and free up time for more valuable pursuits.

- **Shared sense of identity, unity, and trust:** Family offices can play a critical role in fostering a shared vision and sense of identity within a family. They can help facilitate or identify outside experts to facilitate family discussions around shared values, family history and long-term goals, and provide a framework for making decisions that align with these. By facilitating the creation of a shared family mission statement or vision statement, family offices can help promote a sense of unity and purpose across multiple generations. In addition, family offices can help build trust and collaboration within the family by facilitating regular two-way communication between the family enterprise and the family, including providing a platform for sharing information about the business(es), investments, and assets.

- **Supporting the community of family members:** Family offices can offer services to support their clients in managing the family community and family communication to foster unity and a shared purpose. This can be achieved through event management for family meetings and gatherings, including venue selection, guest list management and on-site coordination. This is particularly relevant for larger families, where the logistics of getting everybody together is challenging. In addition, family offices can help manage communication channels between family members, often serving as a neutral third party to ensure that everyone is kept informed about family news and celebrations. These services can include the creation of regular newsletters, scheduling and hosting family meetings and establishing and overseeing a secure digital platform or intranet.

- **Family concierge services:** Family offices can offer concierge services that provide high-level logistical and operational assistance. These services can include personal services such as travel arrangements, event planning and personal shopping as well as asset-related services such as managing aircraft and yachts, home management and bill paying. The goal is to take care of the details of the client's daily life so he or she can focus on their business and personal priorities. The concierge team is often comprised of experienced professionals who have a deep

understanding of their client's needs and preferences, so that they can offer a highly tailored and personalized service, which evidently is a lot more obvious in the case of a single family office but is also offered by multi-family offices.

- **Act as a sounding board on family issues:** Family offices can play an important role as a neutral sounding board for individual family members. By providing a confidential and non-judgmental space for family members to discuss their concerns, family offices can help facilitate open and honest communication. This can be especially important in situations where family dynamics or conflicts may make it difficult for family members to communicate directly with one another. Family offices can act as a trusted advisor, providing guidance and support to individual family members as needed. It is important to recognize that family office professionals typically serve multiple family members, and therefore it is critical that they remain objective and neutral. By serving as a sounding board, they can bring solutions, outside expertise or resolution to issues presented to them.

What do we own?

The second pillar relates to your assets and liabilities as well as the cash flow within your family enterprise ecosystem. The family office supports this second pillar as the vehicle which preserves and, hopefully, grows your family's financial wealth. Its objective is twofold: first, to provide the financial means for current generations to maintain their expected standard of living and pursue their various interests and, second, to safeguard family wealth for future generations.

Within the scope of financial capital – after the owners define their vision and objectives for their financial wealth – the family office can help develop a strategy and execute the management of assets. The family office can find the best way to manage the portfolio of assets, from businesses and investments to property and other high-value tangible assets such as art collections, yachts, aircraft, and collectibles. It also ensures the diversification of wealth across different asset classes, implements investment strategies, ensures that family entities have sufficient liquidity, oversees budgeting and cash flow, approves and executes transactions for the family, manages all the risks and exposure of family investments, provides consolidated reporting, and attends to opaque and often complex tax and legal matters.

Whether in-house or outsourced, the services that fall under this pillar must be carefully chosen based on the circumstances and needs of your entire family. For some families, this means agreeing to pool financial resources for greater efficiency and performance. For other families, it could require careful orchestration that mixes individual strategies and services for some family members with a collective approach in other areas.

Again, there is no right or wrong approach when it comes to the services that the family office provides but, with the future financial health of the family at stake, it is important that the focus of your family office reflect the true complexity and reality of your entire ecosystem and the people in it.

- **Investments:** Family offices are crucial for managing the investment portfolios and asset allocation choices of affluent families with the goal of preserving their wealth and creating a legacy for future generations. One of their primary responsibilities is to ensure the family develops an investment policy statement (IPS) that outlines the investment objectives, risk tolerance and asset allocation strategies. An IPS is created by the owners to reflect their views and goals. It can be developed by the representative owners' council or the investment committee or by the owners collectively. We will go into this topic in more depth in the "Organization" chapter. Regardless of where the document is drafted, the owners approve, and the family office executes. The family office also works closely with the family to understand their financial goals, investment preferences, and constraints. Family offices use their expertise to design a diversified investment portfolio that aligns with the family's investment objectives, risk tolerance, cash flow, budgeting, and liquidity needs. They are responsible for selecting and managing investments in various asset classes including equities, fixed income, alternative investments, commodities, real estate, cash and cash equivalents. In addition to investment management, family offices are also responsible for managing high-value assets such as art collections, yachts, aircraft, property, and collectibles. They work with specialized professionals to ensure that these assets are managed effectively, and that the family's overall wealth is preserved and grown over time in a way that is tailored to each family's unique goals.

- **Finance:** Family offices are responsible for managing a broad range of financial services for affluent families and ensuring that all legal and regulatory requirements are met. One of their primary responsibilities is accounting and bill payments. Family offices manage the family's accounts payable, ensuring that bills are paid on time and accurately. They also manage the family's accounts receivable, ensuring that all incoming payments are correctly recorded and deposited. Tax planning and compliance are another essential aspect of the services provided by family offices. They work with specialized professionals such as tax attorneys and accountants to create tax-efficient strategies that help the family reduce tax liability. Family offices ensure that the family's tax returns are prepared accurately and filed on time, meeting all legal and regulatory requirements.

Trust administration is also an important family office function. They manage trusts established by the family, according to the trust's terms and in line with any legal and regulatory requirements. Family offices work closely with trustees, beneficiaries and legal professionals to ensure that trust assets are protected and managed effectively. Information system management is another critical responsibility of family offices, ensuring that the family's financial information is secure and up to date. Family offices use advanced software systems to manage financial data, track investments, and monitor financial performance. They also ensure that the family's financial data is easily accessible to authorized family members and advisors.

Finally, consolidated reporting is an essential family office service. Family offices provide regular financial reports to the family, summarizing all investment activities, income, expenses and financial performance across all accounts and investments. Consolidated reporting allows the family to have a clear overview of their financial situation, which is essential for making informed decisions about their finances.

Overview of different asset classes

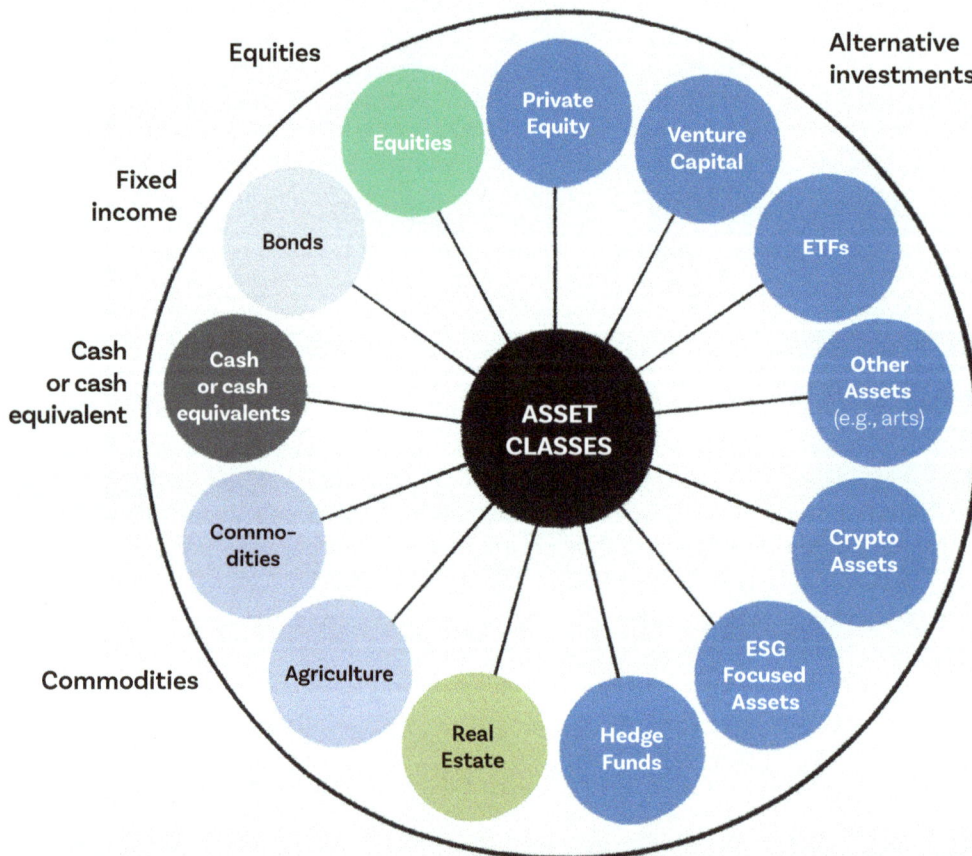

Equities

Alternative investments

Fixed income

Cash or cash equivalent

Commodities

Private Equity
Equities
Venture Capital
ETFs
Bonds
Other Assets (e.g., arts)
Cash or cash equivalents
ASSET CLASSES
Crypto Assets
Commodities
ESG Focused Assets
Agriculture
Real Estate
Hedge Funds

Some of the most common asset classes include:

- **Equities:** Equities, also known as stocks or shares, represent ownership in companies. Equity investors have the potential to earn returns through stock price appreciation and dividends.
- **Fixed Income:** Fixed income investments include bonds, which are debt instruments issued by governments or corporations. Investors earn interest income and receive principal repayment at maturity.
- **Real Estate:** Real estate investments include residential and commercial properties, as well as real estate investment trusts (REITs). Real estate investments offer the potential for rental income and price appreciation.
- **Alternative Investments:** Alternative investments include hedge funds, private equity, venture capital, and commodities. These investments typically have lower liquidity and higher risk than traditional asset classes.
- **Commodities:** Commodities are raw materials or primary agricultural products that are traded on exchanges. Examples of commodities include gold, silver, crude oil, natural gas, wheat, corn and soybeans.
- **Cash and Cash Equivalents:** Cash and cash equivalents are short-term investments that include savings accounts, money market funds and certificates of deposit (CDs). These investments offer low risk and low returns.

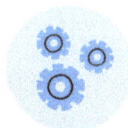

How do we function?

This third pillar is focused on services that help ensure the family enterprise ecosystem is well-structured and governed, accountable, ethical, and responsible. It might be tempting to focus solely on what happens to the money, but the future health and prosperity of your family and its ecosystem will very much depend, in the end, on the quality of its holistic governance structures and the robustness of processes for family decision-making and behavior.

The family office can become a powerful platform to strengthen the family enterprise ecosystem as a sustainable, well-managed institution by helping to uphold a holistically aligned family, ownership, business, and investment governance.

At the same time, the family office can perform day-to-day administrative tasks for the family, acting as an institutional hub and glue for the ecosystem. Part of this role could include the housing and archiving of important documents relating to legal and tax affairs, compliance as well as key governance documents relating to the family, businesses, ownership and investments. And, importantly, the family office can act as a safe and fair conduit for neutral and effective communication between the family.

- **Effective, efficient, and coordinated governance:** Family offices play a vital role in supporting families and owners in ensuring effective and efficient governance of the wider family enterprise ecosystem, as well as to ensure that all aspects of governance across the system – including the family, ownership, businesses, and investments – are aligned and coordinated. This is particularly important in larger and more complex systems. For example, the family council may ask the family office to support them to develop the foundations of family governance, including the necessary protocols for decision-making. The owners' council can also ask the family office to support them as they establish and oversee their ownership governance, which is essential if the system involves multiple shareholders and multiple entities, possibly being exposed to multiple jurisdictions, among many other complexities. Additionally, family offices can assist with succession planning, ensuring that there is a clear and well-communicated plan for transferring ownership and leadership to the next generation. One of the challenges in managing a family enterprise ecosystem is ensuring cohesion between different governance activities. Family offices can help families develop a shared vision for the future, identify key priorities, and develop strategies for achieving their goals in a way that is aligned with the family's values. By taking a holistic approach to governance, family offices can help families build a robust and sustainable ecosystem that will endure for generations to come.

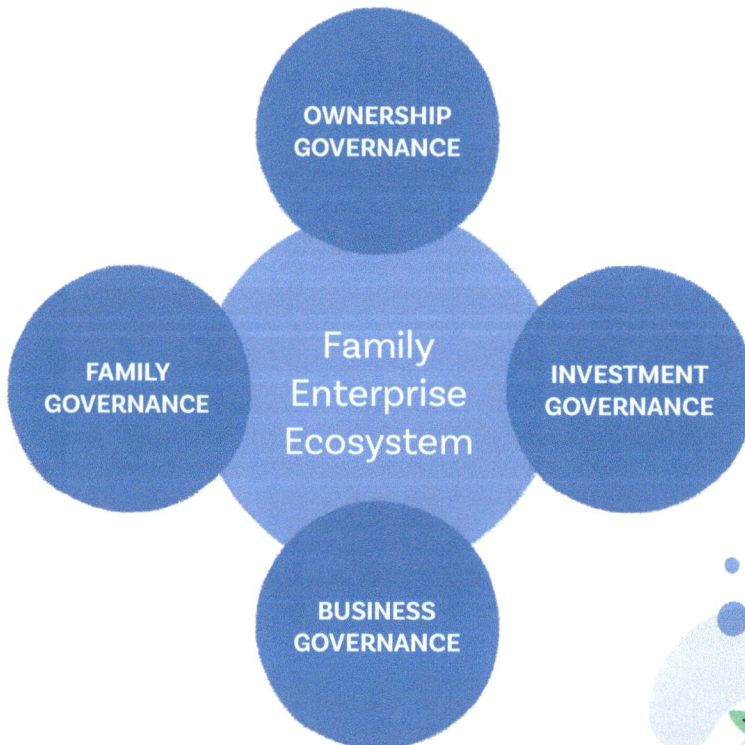

- **Manage legal and tax matters:** The management of legal and tax aspects is a crucial area of focus for family offices. The ever-changing legal and tax landscape requires constant attention and expertise. Family offices play a critical role in ensuring compliance and mitigating risks. This is particularly important for larger and more complex family enterprise ecosystems with exposure to multiple jurisdictions. By providing strategic advice and guidance, family offices can help families navigate complex legal and tax issues, including tax planning, estate planning and philanthropic giving. Furthermore, family offices can assist in the management of legal risks, including ensuring compliance with relevant regulations and laws. By managing legal and tax matters effectively, family offices can help ensure the long-term financial security of the family and its assets, while also preserving their legacy and values.

- **Trusteeship services:** Trusteeship services are a critical function of a family office. These services ensure that the assets and wealth of a family are properly managed and protected. A trustee is a fiduciary who is responsible for managing and distributing assets according to the terms of a trust. A family office can provide trustee fiduciary services, act as an agent for trustee compliance and advise on distributive duties. They can also provide investment and beneficiary education, cost analysis and negotiation of trustee fees, selection and training of trustees and protectors, beneficiary education and mentoring, and estate administration. These services are essential for ensuring that a family's wealth is preserved and passed down to future generations in the optimal way.

- **Liability management:** Liability management is another critical service offered by a family office. These services are designed to protect a family's assets and mitigate risks. A family office can perform a trustee liability audit, assess property and casualty insurance, analyze life insurance coverage, and provide specialty practice lines of insurance. They can also assist with personal security, collectibles inventory, appraisal, and protection, as well as carrier solvency reporting. These services help ensure that a family's wealth is protected from potential liabilities and risks. By managing these risks effectively, a family can maintain its financial security and ensure that its assets are preserved for future generations.

- **Administrative services:** The administrative role of a family office is critical to the success of the family enterprise ecosystem. One key aspect of this role is the management of important documents, including housing and archiving them in a secure and organized manner. Family offices may also oversee bookkeeping, tracking financial transactions and preparing financial reports. Additionally, they can manage daily operations such as sorting mail and managing IT systems. Office management is another area where family offices can provide support, such as overseeing office space and staffing.

Furthermore, family offices can handle various types of insurance and coordinate risk management activities. By managing administrative tasks effectively, family offices can free up time and resources for family members to focus on their core activities and interests.

What is our role in society and our impact on the environment?

The fourth pillar addresses the family's impact on society and the environment. In an ideal world, this means helping the family to fulfill its goals, responsibilities and purpose in terms of social and environmental impact. Prosperous, enterprising families play a significant role in shaping the future of their communities, wider society, and the planet, either through their business activities, impact investments or philanthropic initiatives. The family office can provide a useful platform to harmonize and unify these activities into a collective impact strategy that can both bring the family together while also enhancing outcomes.

In the award-winning predecessor to this book, the *Family Philanthropy Navigator* (2020), families were able to explore the vital role they have played throughout history and will continue to play as stewards of workforces, communities, society, and the planet. This included a step-by-step guide and practical tool for families to navigate their own effective and impactful philanthropic journey, no matter the size or scope of their ambitions or interests. While many families manage their philanthropic activities separately and outside the core businesses and family office, via a family foundation, some families leverage their family office to help them bring all their social and environmental ambitions under one roof to be coordinated in a professional, impact-driven, and efficient way.

Key to the vision of the family office overseeing family social impact is ensuring a cohesive, holistic, and deliberate approach to ensure that your family can have the greatest positive impact possible on society and the environment. The family office can play a key role here to support your family with its specific social impact activities, such as impact investing or philanthropy. It could even have a role in aligning and coordinating the company's ESG or corporate social responsibility strategy with the family's overall social impact goals. It can become a platform to design and deliver a cohesive and collective strategy to maximize family impact that encompasses the entire family ecosystem, in line with its goals and purpose as a responsible institution. Finally, the family office, in its administrative capacity, could help your family become more sustainable by exploring how to reduce its carbon footprint or adopt greener, fairer practices across the family enterprise ecosystem.

- **ESG focus of business and investment activities:** As awareness and concern for environmental, social, and governance (ESG) issues continue to rise, the role of family offices in managing their ESG activities has become increasingly important. Family offices can help to ensure that businesses the family is involved with operate in line with the family's purpose and values, and in an environmentally and socially responsible manner. This can include setting standards for sustainable business practices, conducting ESG due diligence, and monitoring and reporting on ESG performance. Additionally, family offices, in managing the family's investment activities, can deploy asset allocation strategies that are aligned with the family's investment principles and the desired ESG impact. Family offices can identify investment opportunities that align with the family's values and ESG goals, while also delivering competitive financial returns. By managing the family's ESG activities effectively, family offices can foster the long-term financial security of the family, while contributing to a more sustainable and just society.

- **Philanthropic activities:** Family offices can serve as an ideal platform for managing a family's philanthropic activities, not only to give back to society but also to manage the family's legacy across generations and to ensure that the family's giving activities are aligned with the investments. Philanthropy can be a powerful tool for families to proactively express their values and make a positive impact on society. However, managing philanthropic activities can be complex and time-consuming. Family offices can offer valuable support in this area, through services such as strategic planning, program development, grant-making and impact evaluation. Additionally, family offices can help align philanthropic activities with the family's values and legacy, ensuring that the family's philanthropic efforts are consistent with its purpose and vision.

- **Help the family in their personal sustainability / ESG efforts:** The role of the family office can extend beyond financial management and investment activities to include a focus on helping the family become more sustainable. Family offices can help families develop and implement sustainability strategies that promote responsible living and consumption, as well as investment practices. This can include developing environmentally friendly policies and procedures for family homes and businesses.

- **Managing reputational capital:** In today's fast-paced and increasingly transparent world with 24/7 digital access, a family's reputation can be damaged in an instant, and it can take years to recover. Family offices can help families protect and enhance their reputation by developing and implementing strategies that promote responsible behavior and ethical business practices. This can include monitoring the media for mentions of the family, managing social media accounts and developing crisis management plans to respond to any negative publicity or reputational threats. Family offices can also provide guidance and support to family members on how to conduct themselves in the public eye and ensure that their actions align with the family's values and principles. By managing the family's reputational capital effectively, family offices can help families maintain their credibility and integrity, which is critical for the success of their businesses, investments, and philanthropic activities.

This high-level overview of services is meant to provide you and your family some guidance in your reflection processes when it comes to which services are most valuable to you. It is not meant as an exhaustive list and we consciously chose not to go into too much technical detail on each one of them at this stage.

A few important reminders before we proceed:

1. **A family office does not have to include all these services.**
   It is important that you carefully consider which ones are important you and your family. This should be inspired by your reflections during the previous chapters with respect to your needs as well as the complexities of your family enterprise ecosystem.
2. **The range of services that you and your family need will change and evolve over time.**
   You should therefore carefully revisit any existing services and consider which ones you might wish to remove, change or add. Important inflections points for such major strategy reviews include generational transitions, changes in ownership, liquidity events, geographic shifts, or other larger transformations of your system.

STRATEGIC CHOICES

When considering the needs of your family and how that will influence the focus of your family office, we believe it is helpful to reflect on the following set of strategic choices. These choices will help to frame your discussions and decisions by illustrating an array of trade-offs, challenges, risks, limitations, options and opportunities.

We would emphasize two points at this stage of the voyage. One, there is no one-size-fits-all solution here; each family is unique and, therefore, each family office is unique. And two, this is a journey and your responses to each of these strategic choices will change depending on where you are on that journey.

PURELY FINANCIALLY FOCUSED		BROADER FOCUS

The family office is focused on managing the financial aspects of the family

The purpose and the focus of your family office will change over time and across generations. It is important to take a decision as to whether you wish your family office to have a purely financial mandate or whether you want your family office to take a broader and more holistic approach to managing total family wealth.

Reflect on the following questions:

- *Is the exclusive purpose of your family office to manage the family's financial wealth or should it also be taking care of other aspects?*
- *How well are the various aspects of your total family wealth taken care of today and where might you need some support? Might the various governance bodies (e.g., family council, ownership council, philanthropic leadership team, etc.) benefit from some support from the family office?*

The family office is focused on serving the family across the wider spectrum of Total Family Wealth

CENTRAL POSITIONING

PERIPHERAL POSITIONING

Family office positioned at the core of the family enterprise ecosystem, holding everything together

Family office sitting on the periphery of the family enterprise ecosystem, with a narrow focus, and not strategically contributing to or necessarily aligned with all other activities

For some families, it is important to create a family office structure that sits at the heart of the family enterprise system and plays an orchestrating role. We call this a centralized approach. For other families, family office services might be best kept on the periphery of the system and simply focus on ancillary services. We refer to this approach as peripheral.

To explore this spectrum of possibilities in the context of your own family, consider the following questions:

- *How central do you want your family office and its services to be within the system?*
- *Do you want the family office to play an orchestrating role in your family enterprise ecosystem to ensure alignment across all activities, or do you prefer that the family office to be kept separate from the other activities?*
- *Could some services be provided on an ad hoc basis?*
- *What are the benefits and costs of a centralized approach for your family?*

IN-HOUSE	←•••••••→	OUTSOURCED

Managing services from within the family office

Some families have many capabilities across their ecosystems which can be drawn on to manage key elements of the family office in-house. Our experience, however, shows that it is worth examining options outside of the family's castle walls to tap into independent, professional expertise that, if managed and governed well, can yield better results.

Consider the following questions:

- *What activities do you think would be best taken care of from within the family office?*
- *Do you have the management capabilities and owner-oversight experience for a team to execute these services in-house?*
- *Which services do you need to be closely managed (for example, for privacy reasons)?*
- *Which services do you need highly customized and tailored?*
- *From a cost-benefit perspective, which services should you offer in-house versus outsource?*
- *How cost-sensitive are you and your family?*

Outsourcing services to partners outside the family office

Central versus peripheral approach

Finding the right balance in family office service provision

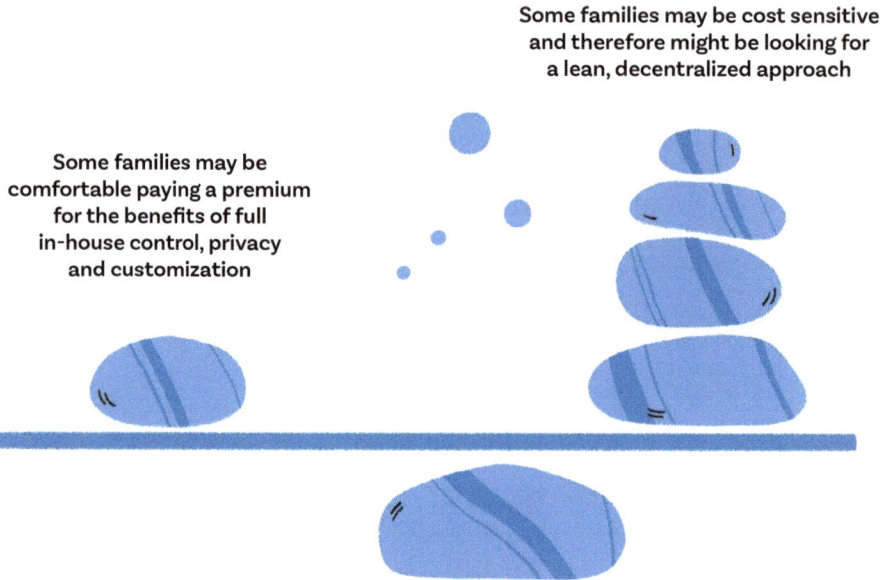

Some families may be cost sensitive and therefore might be looking for a lean, decentralized approach

Some families may be comfortable paying a premium for the benefits of full in-house control, privacy and customization

Benefits of in-house vs. outsourcing

Benefits of in-house services	Benefits of outsourced services
• Enhanced confidentiality and privacy. • Trusted and independent advice. • Family wealth is managed in a consolidated manner. • Tailored skill development to meet the family's specific needs. • The family maintains greater control over its wealth. • Investment knowledge is kept within the family. • Optimal goal agreement is assured and conflicts of interest with external providers are avoided.	• Improved staff productivity and reduced overhead costs. • Economies of scale, particularly for high-value professional services, leading to lower prices for related services. • Objective advice from highly specialized professionals. • Outsourcing investment management can help defend the family office's regulatory independence by allowing external providers to make investment decisions. • Family office directors can conduct due diligence and continuous monitoring to ensure performance and security against risk.

SHORT-TERM		LONG-TERM

The family office provides services that are relevant in the short-term

It is easy to race ahead in establishing the core elements of a family office. In some instances, families establish an informally structured vehicle that provides a narrow set of services because they require these services urgently. In other instances, they might set up something more substantial without reflecting carefully on the bigger picture. However, while there are very legitimate reasons for focusing on the short-term, many families benefit from gazing into the future and asking themselves where they want to be in one or two generations' time.

The family office develops services that are relevant in the long-term

Reflect on the following questions:

- *Do you have urgent needs that must be addressed?*
- *Can some elements be left for later?*
- *Where are you on your journey as a family? Do you want the family office to focus on the needs of the current generation?*
- *Do you have a longer-term view in mind to cater for multiple generations?*
- *How complex or simple are your family's needs?*
- *How will these reflections impact the focus of your family office?*

ACTIVITIES

Now that you have explored the four main pillars of the focus of the family office and delved into some of the key strategic choices that might influence that focus, it is time to define the scope and type of services that you would like your family office to manage at this moment in time.

To help you achieve this, we have devised the following structured activities for you and your family to work on together. As with all the activities in the previous chapters, allocate the necessary time and create the right setting for the kind of open, honest and exploratory discussions that are required to come to a clear, shared point of view.

> **Family Office Navigator questions:**
>
> - What will be the core activities and services of our family office?
> - Which ones are strategic?

ACTIVITY 1:
MAKING SENSE OF YOUR STRATEGIC CHOICES

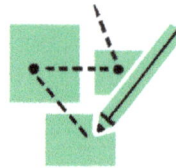

In this activity, we will take a look at your family's responses to the strategic choices that we presented earlier in this chapter and help you translate that information in the context of the focus of your family office.
How do your answers to those choices influence and shape your collective view with respect to the different services that your family office should be focusing on?

Gather your family to review the answers and choices you came to, while moving through the strategic choices which we have elaborated on earlier in this chapter:

- **Purely financially-focused vs more broadly focused**
- **Central vs peripheral**
- **In-house vs outsourced**
- **Short-term vs long-term**

Step 1

Individually, go through these strategic choices and reflect on your point of view on each of them. The following questions might help you during this reflection:

- **Which strategic choices are more relevant or important for you than others?**
- **What are your reasons for choosing one way or another?**

Step 2

Gather as a family and present your perspectives on each of these strategic choices, and discuss the following:

- **What are the differences of opinion for each choice?**
- **Where do you share common ground for each choice?**
- **Can you see an overarching narrative forming around your answers?**

Try to compare notes and, ideally, agree on a shared position for each strategic choice. If there is too much dissonance or it is difficult to agree, it may be worth considering how to reflect that in your choice of family office services. Does the family office need to cater to different needs and individuals? Could there be some structural choices that you can make in order to accommodate the different wishes and needs of individuals within the family (for example, selecting the single "multi" family office as a model).

ACTIVITY 2:
DEFINING YOUR FAMILY OFFICE SERVICES

This activity is focused on making choices around the specific services that you deem essential for your family office in the short-, mid-, and long-term. We will also reflect on how you deal with these aspects at the moment and whether those services are strategic or not, thus informing whether they should be handled in-house or not.

Here, again, is the list of family office services which we already introduced earlier in this chapter, to serve as a reference for this exercise.

Potential focus areas for family office services

The four pillars of family office services	Who are we as a family?	What do we own?	How do we function?	What is our role in society and our impact on the environment?
Family office orientation	*Family office services that help family members individually flourish and that help us remain an informed, united and harmonious family*	*Family office services that help us manage assets, liabilities, and cash flow within our family enterprise ecosystem*	*Family office services that help us ensure effective and cohesive governance and decision-making across all aspects of our family enterprise ecosystem*	*Family office services that help us ensure that we have the most positive impact on society and the environment*
Specific focus areas for the family office	**Human Capital:** • Education of family members broadly (e.g., funding for school) • Develop family members to capably serve the family enterprise (e.g., owner preparation, board member preparation) • Help family members in their professional development (e.g., leadership development, career building) • Ensure physical & psychological health (e.g., insurance, special treatments, support in difficult times) **Social Capital:** • Support the family in building a shared vision and a shared sense of identity • Foster good relationships, unity and trust across the family • Support the family community (family meetings, events, communication, etc.) • Provide family concierge services • Act as a sounding board regarding family issues and solutions	**Financial Capital:** • Execute the owners' investment strategy and policies • Ensure sufficient diversification of assets according to the investment policy • Help the family manage risk exposure • Manage the portfolio of assets, including businesses, investments, properties and other high-value assets (e.g., art, yachts, aircraft, collectibles) • Manage liquidity needs (for family and business entities) • Oversee budgeting & cash flow of the family • Handle liability management • Approve and execute transactions • Manage accounting and bill paying for the family • Provide tax planning and compliance for the family • Conduct wealth transfer planning • Offer regular, consolidated reporting for the family	• Support the family in ensuring effective and efficient governance for the family, ownership, business and investments • Support the family in continuity and succession matters • Manage the legal and tax matters of the family • Provide trusteeship services • House and archive various documents (e.g., history, ownership, legal, tax, compliance) • Perform administrative tasks for the family enterprise ecosystem (e.g., bookkeeping, mail, IT, office management) • Facilitate effective and transparent, two-way communication between the family and the enterprise	• Support the family with executing their philanthropic and overall social impact activities • Help the family develop a cohesive strategy across all the businesses, investing and philanthropic activities to maximize ESG impact (typically at the direction of the owners' council or family council) • Help the family in their personal sustainability initiatives and attendant lifestyle transitions • Help the family preserve and nurture its reputational capital through its impact activities

Step 1

Individually, go through this table and reflect on each element:

• What needs and complexities did you identify in the "Charting Y our Course" chapter? These might help you identify possible family office services.
• Are there any areas where you have a pressing need or special interest?
• Which of these four major areas are important to you and your family today, and why?

Step 2

Using the previous table as a reference, fill out the following table individually, bearing in mind the following questions:

• Which of these services are important for you and your family?
• How important are each of those services in the short-, mid-, and long-term? You might want to define yourself what these different timeframes mean in your family system. We suggest "short-term" being 1-3 years, 3-10 years for "mid-term" and "long-term" as 10+ years.
• How are these services taken care of at the moment, if at all?
• Which of these services do you think should be handled in-house and which could be outsourced?

Services of interest	Are these services relevant for you in the short (1 3 y), mid- (3-10 y) or long-term (10+ y)?			How is this managed / taken care of today? (if not at all, leave blank)	Is this something you would rather see taken care of in-house by the FO, or could this also be outsourced as part of a hybrid FO?
	Short	Mid	Long		
	☐	☐	☐		
	☐	☐	☐		
	☐	☐	☐		
	☐	☐	☐		
	☐	☐	☐		
	☐	☐	☐		
	☐	☐	☐		
	☐	☐	☐		
	☐	☐	☐		
	☐	☐	☐		
	☐	☐	☐		

Step 3

Come together as a family to review your individual responses and work towards a common, defined set of services for your family office. This step may take a while, but it will genuinely be worth it, both in creating greater understanding and shared purpose within your family.

A few things to keep in mind at this stage:

- You do not have to launch all the desired services at once. Start with the most important, core services and initiate your journey. Setting up a family office is, like any new venture, a learning process in itself. Therefore, it is a lot easier to get going with a small, focused approach in which you do not get lost in too much complexity.
- The more services you consider, the more costly the family office setup will likely be. Therefore, it is also smart to start small and learn about which services you really need and which ones you could be dealing with in a different, more cost-effective way.

CONCLUSION

All family offices need a defined focus to deliver an effective and efficient range of services that will support and nurture a strong and sustainable family enterprise ecosystem, no matter how far-reaching and complex, or basic and narrow those services might be.

By this stage of the *Family Office Navigator*, you have come to a greater appreciation of the range of services a family office can provide, and how those services support the preservation and development of the family's total family wealth and ecosystem, in line with its purpose. You have also considered the strategic choices that frame the focus of your family office, depending on the complexity of your ecosystem and where your family is on its own unique journey.

Finally, you have worked with your family to define and prioritize the services that you would like your family office to focus on at this moment in time, fully aware that the demands on the family office are likely to change over time as your family enterprise ecosystem evolves.

With this crucial information, we will now progress to the next chapter in the *Navigator* – organizing your family office. In this chapter, we will delve into the possible governance, structures, processes, and resources of your family office, and how those should be managed in relation to your needs and circumstances, and how these elements can change over time. We will look at some existing models, archetypal examples and best practices, sharing insights and expertise from family office professionals and families at different stages of their journeys with various degrees of complexity.

Through this pivotal part of our journey, we will help you bring the direction, purpose, and focus of your family office to life, so that you can embark with confidence and clarity on your family office journey - or strike off boldly in a new direction.

CHAPTER 5

ORGANIZING YOUR FAMILY OFFICE

Organizing your family office to master the present and pave the way for an impactful aspirational future.

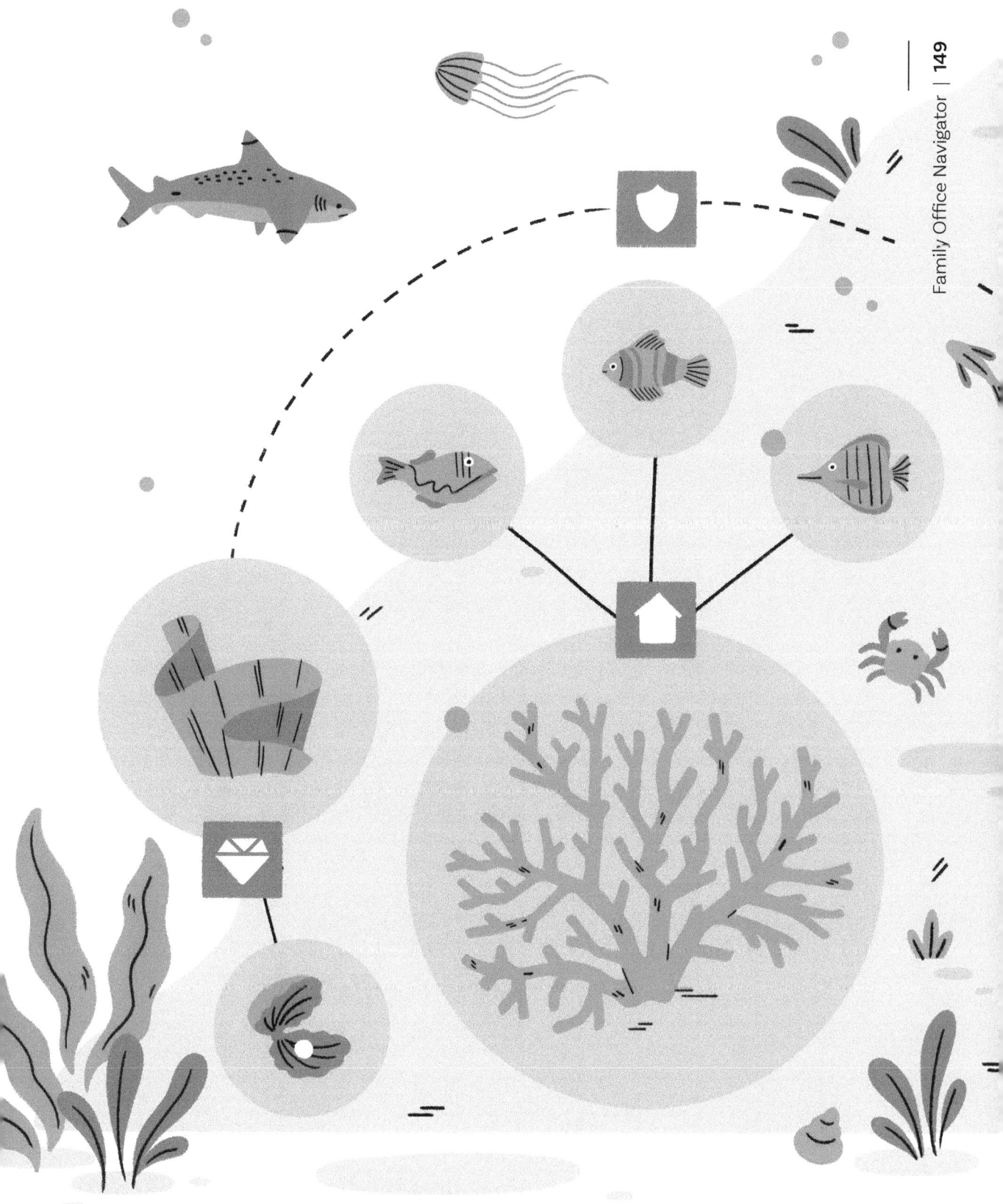

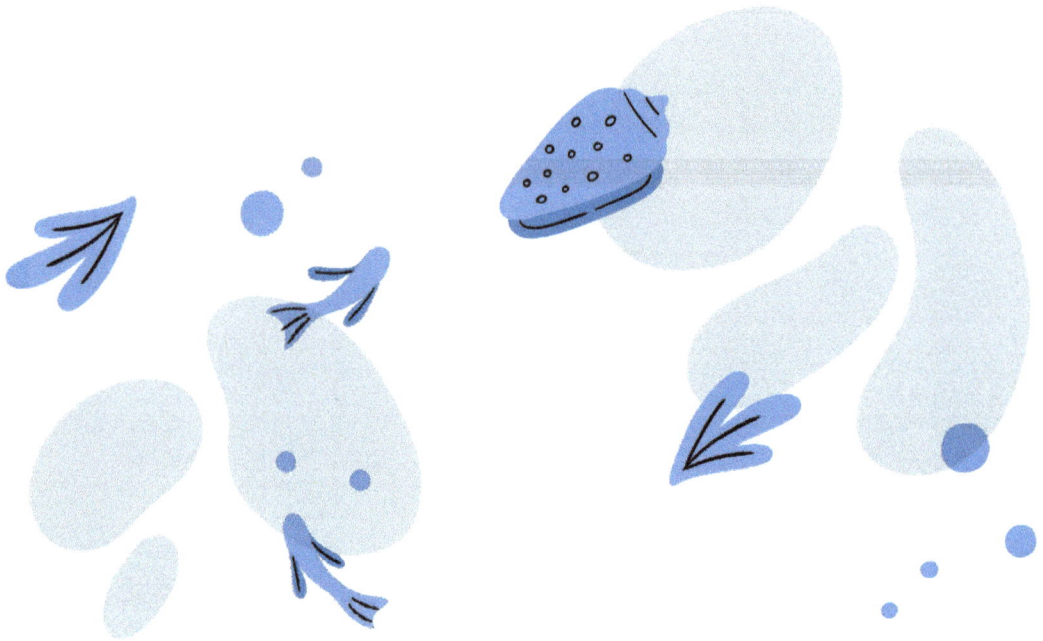

Status quo of our
family enterprise ecosystem

Aspirations for the future of
our family enterprise ecosystem

OUR FAMILY MANIFESTO

PURPOSE OF
OUR FAMILY OFFICE

FOCUS OF OUR FAMILY OFFICE

| Who we are | What we own | How we function | Our impact on society and the environment |

ORGANIZATION OF OUR FAMILY OFFICE

| Structure | Resources | Governance and monitoring |

LAYING THE CORNERSTONE

How should we organize our family office to ensure that it fulfills its purpose? What structures can we put in place to help us manage our family enterprise in its current form, as well as its future incarnations? How can we deliver services to the family in the most effective, efficient and impactful way?

In this section of the *Family Office Navigator*, we focus on the three key areas of organizing a family office:

Structure   **Resources**   **Governance and monitoring**

First, we will examine the different structures of family offices and explore what might work best for you and your family. Choosing the right structure is the cornerstone of a successful family office. Second, we will review the types of resources that are essential to meeting your family's needs. Strategic allocation of resources is pivotal in the realm of family offices. Taking a holistic approach to resource management will enable you to streamline operations. Then, we will answer a series of important questions on governance & monitoring: How do we govern the family office? What rules, processes, policies will help us? How will we connect the family office governance with other mechanisms in the system? How do we measure our family office performance? What are our metrics of success? Are these aligned with our family manifesto and purpose? How do we know that we are successful?

In the interest of brevity, we will not delve into each area in too much depth but we encourage you to consult the list of resources given at the end of the book if you wish to learn about the more technical aspects involved in organizing a family office.

Remember your purpose

Throughout your family office journey, do not lose sight of your purpose as a family enterprise and be prepared to revisit and reflect on it at different stages. The nature of your purpose is key for designing – or redesigning – the organizational structure of your family office. Whether your primary goal is to manage your liquidity or to manage other aspects of your total family wealth, keep in mind the motivations that led you to establish your family office as you progress through this section of the *Navigator*.

STRUCTURE

Setting the scene

What types of family offices exist, and which one fits our family's situation and needs best? What do we need to consider when choosing the right family office structure? What are the pros and cons of the different structures? What do we need to consider when it comes to assessing multi family offices (MFOs)? Does it make economic sense for us to set up our own single family office (SFO)? How will we go about setting up our family office? Where should it be located?

Several key factors will inevitably drive the discussion around these questions, including your total family wealth, the range of issues that you wish your family office to handle, the complexity of your family (size, geographic proximity, etc.), the size and complexity of your assets, the wish or need for highly personalized services, or a strong desire or need for confidentiality.

Getting the structure of your family office right at this stage is a crucial step. It is worthwhile taking the necessary time to understand the various structures, their pros and cons and how they align with the purpose and focus of your family office, before discussing how to proceed.

In the following chapter, we will demystify the most important technicalities and jargon, discuss the big questions and provide clear guidance so that you and your family can take the decisions necessary to move forward.

Family office archetypes

Earlier in the book, we introduced various types of family offices that exist. By now you probably agree with us when we say that there is no one-size-fits-all model for the family office. Every family enterprise ecosystem is unique, constantly evolving over time. Families have their specific circumstances which influence the type of family office that might work best.

Here is a recap of the main family office archetypes, which will serve as a basis for deciding on the right structure for you and your family.

An overview of family office archetypes

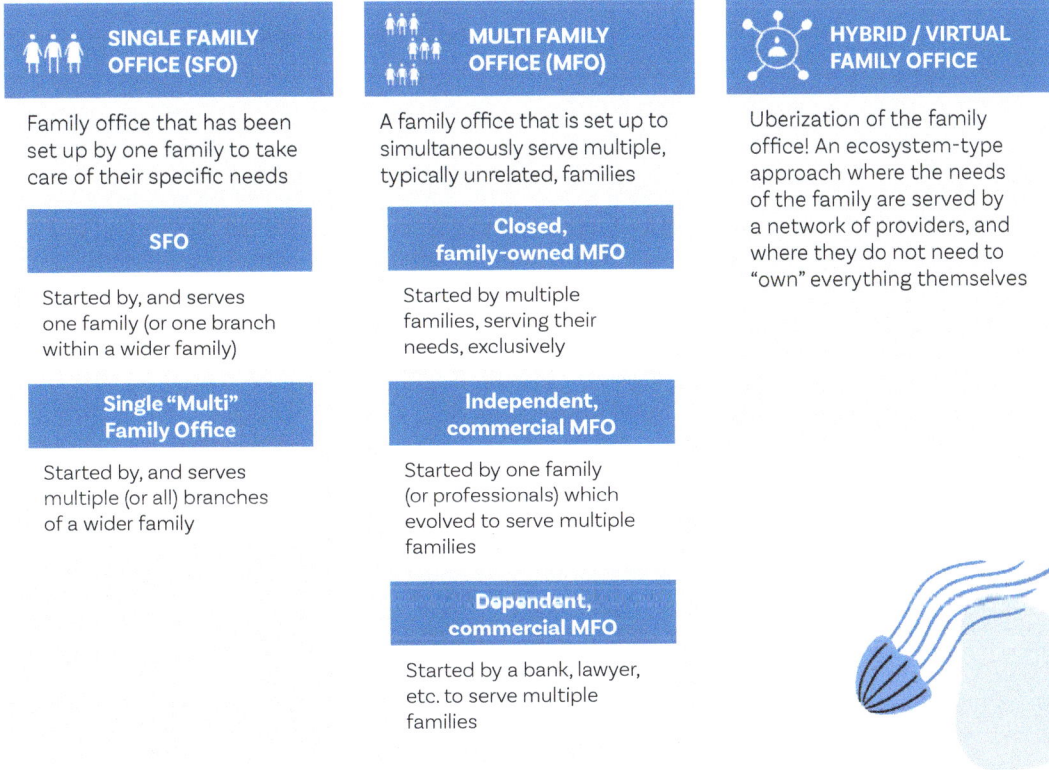

SINGLE FAMILY OFFICE (SFO)

Family office that has been set up by one family to take care of their specific needs

SFO

Started by, and serves one family (or one branch within a wider family)

Single "Multi" Family Office

Started by, and serves multiple (or all) branches of a wider family

MULTI FAMILY OFFICE (MFO)

A family office that is set up to simultaneously serve multiple, typically unrelated, families

Closed, family-owned MFO

Started by multiple families, serving their needs, exclusively

Independent, commercial MFO

Started by one family (or professionals) which evolved to serve multiple families

Dependent, commercial MFO

Started by a bank, lawyer, etc. to serve multiple families

HYBRID / VIRTUAL FAMILY OFFICE

Uberization of the family office! An ecosystem-type approach where the needs of the family are served by a network of providers, and where they do not need to "own" everything themselves

The Single Family Office (SFO)

The single family office is dedicated to a single affluent family with the mandate of managing their human-, social- and financial capital, as well as other affairs in the family enterprise ecosystem. Its objective is to continue the family's legacy for generations to come. This approach provides a centralized solution for the family's wealth management needs and offers a high degree of privacy, control, and customization. SFOs usually require significant financial resources to establish and maintain, making them accessible and applicable only to ultra-high net worth families.

Within the category of SFOs, we see variations, such as the single "multi" family office, which is started by and serves multiple branches of a wider family. While this model offers many shared activities and services, it also proposes tailored services branch-by-branch, possibly even tailored asset allocation or philanthropy management, depending on the setup. The single "multi" family office can be seen as a hybrid structure that combines some of the benefits of a single family office and a multi family office (see next definition). Keeping it within the same family, while allowing each branch to access customized services that might not be of interest to overlap other branches in the wider family, has its advantages.

The Multi Family Office (MFO)

This is a family office that has been set up to serve multiple, typically unrelated families. Within this category, there are also variations. One is what we call the *closed, family-owned multi family office*, which is established by several unrelated families from the beginning and serves their needs exclusively. These might be families that are in business together or trust each other well enough to embark on such a joint venture. Another form of a multi family office is the independent, *commercial multi family office*, which is started by one family but then evolves to serve several unrelated families. The Rockefellers' family office is one such example. It was set up as a single family office and then built on its growing knowledge and expertise in the field to become a *multi family office* serving many affluent families around the world. Finally, there is what we call a *dependent, commercial multi family office*, which is founded by a bank or a professional services firm (a legal or fiduciary firm, for instance) to serve multiple clients / families.

Potential conflicts of interest

Families need to be aware that when they decide to join a multi family office their interests might not always be 100% aligned with those of the third-party owners and managers of that office. While, obviously, they are interested in having happy clients, they are eager to maximize their own income and profits, whereas the family is interested in keeping its costs as low as possible. Another aspect to be mindful of is that bank-bound multi family offices might offer their own products to other clients which, in turn, prevents them from being fully independent and serving the family with the broadest range of investment options. That said, multi family offices bring many advantages, such as access to a larger network and a broad range of expertise. It is important that families that decide to join a multi family office do their homework beforehand, requesting full transparency of any incentive mechanisms and structures.

When doing your due diligence on different MFO providers, you might want to consider the following questions:

Questions to address before you start interacting with MFOs (via desk research or by talking to people in the field)	• Who are they? Do you know any other families that are served by them? What do they say about them? • What information can you find about them that is publicly available? • Is the company part of any specific, reputable networks or organizations? • When were they founded, and by whom? What did their founders do previously, and what is their level of expertise in the domain of family offices? • What type of MFO is it (as per the list and differentiation above)? Has it emerged from an SFO or was it launched as a MFO?

Questions to ask the MFO directly during your interactions	<ul><li>**About their services and value proposition:**<ul><li>What types of services (as per the overview provided in the "Focus" chapter) do they offer and what is their expertise in each of them?</li><li>What are their areas of greatest strength? Any notable recognitions or other credentials they can provide?</li><li>What distinguishes them from their competition?</li></ul></li><li>**Products:**<ul><li>What is their investment process?</li><li>How does the family office decide on its asset allocation?</li><li>How do they measure risk in this context?</li><li>Which tools do they use (risk tools, optimizers)?</li><li>How do they conduct the process with a future client to establish an investment policy statement (IPS)?</li><li>How do they choose their products? (You should request a presentation about their process.)</li><li>Will they use their own products in their investment? What is the performance of those products?</li><li>Do they stock pick? If yes, how do they choose their themes and stocks?</li><li>Do they offer alternative investments?</li><li>What is their analytical process to choose an investment manager?</li><li>Do they have access to institutional-quality products? If yes, how is the investment conducted? What is their level of expertise?</li><li>If applicable: Why are proprietary (investment) products offered? Are such products unavailable in the market? Do they offer a better price or better returns?</li></ul></li><li>**Their clients and client relationship:**<ul><li>How many families and what types of families (size, complexity, assets, locations, wealth creators vs. inheritors, etc.) do they serve today?</li><li>How has their portfolio of clients changed over the past years (additions, losses, shifts, etc.) and why?</li><li>Which of their services do most of the clients use?</li><li>What are their total assets under management (AUM)?</li><li>How have the AUM changed over the past years? Growth of AUM through new clients? Growth of AUM from existing clients? Loss of AUM due to departure of clients?</li><li>Can they provide reference clients who might be willing to provide insights into their work?</li><li>How does their interaction with clients take place? (Form, frequency)</li><li>What is the reporting format for the client? Is there an online dashboard for clients? Can they provide an example report?</li><li>What types of education (workshops, events, research reports, papers, newsletters, etc.) do they offer to their clients?</li></ul></li><li>**About their employees:**<ul><li>How many employees do they have in each of the service areas they offer? Who are the employees in the service areas that you are most interested in?</li><li>How many clients does one client relationship manager typically serve?</li><li>How are the client relationship managers compensated?</li></ul></li><li>**Fees:**<ul><li>What is their fee structure for the various types of services they provide? Ask them to share a list with you. How does this adjust with the amount that they handle per client?</li><li>Do they offer performance-based fees?</li><li>Are there minimum account sizes to enter into a relationship with them?</li><li>What are their sources of income other than advisory fees? Any placement fees for products or deals?</li></ul></li></ul>

Advantages and disadvantages of SFOs vs MFOs

SFO	MFO
• **Customized and tailored services:** An SFO is designed to cater specifically to the needs of one family, allowing for a more customized and tailored approach to managing their wealth. • **Confidentiality and privacy:** The SFO operates solely for one family, providing a high level of confidentiality and privacy for the family as well as its financial information and dealings. • **Direct control:** The family has direct control over the management of their wealth, allowing for a more hands-on approach to investment decision-making. • **Expertise:** An SFO can bring in specialized expertise to address specific needs and challenges facing the family. • **Family first:** An SFO is tailored to one family and does not have to manage the different (sometimes diverging) interests of multiple different families.	• **Access to a wider range of investment opportunities:** MFOs can offer access to a broader range of investment opportunities, as they have a larger pool of resources and expertise to draw on. • **Advanced infrastructure and efficiency:** MFOs can offer their clients a more elaborate infrastructure, including data management, and access to well-proven processes and systems, thus leading to efficiency gains. • **Cost savings:** The shared resources of an MFO can result in cost savings for clients, as the costs of setting up and maintaining the office are spread across multiple families. • **Scale:** MFOs have the advantage of scale when it comes to deal sourcing, infrastructure, access to services as well as the ability to attract and retain top talent. • **Shared resources:** MFOs pool resources and expertise, allowing for a more comprehensive range of services and support for clients. • **Regulatory oversight:** In most jurisdictions, MFOs are regulated by a financial market oversight regime, ensuring aspects such as disclosure and management of conflicts of interest, information technology security and business contingency plans.

SFO	MFO
• **Cost:** SFOs can be expensive to set up and maintain, as the family is responsible for all the costs associated with running the office. In essence, it's owning and running another company with the associated overheads (hiring, training, oversight).	• **Lack of alignment between principal and advisor:** Given the more anonymous nature of the relationship between the family and the employees of the MFO, the risk of limited alignment between them is higher compared to an SFO.
• **High barrier to entry:** The level of wealth required to make an SFO economically viable is substantial.	• **Less personalized attention:** MFOs serve multiple families, so the level of individual attention and customized services may not be as high as with an SFO.
• **Limited resources:** An SFO may have limited resources, as it is serving only one family, making it harder to provide a full range of services. In addition, it might not have access to the best talents in the market.	• **Limited control:** Clients of an MFO have less direct control over the management of their wealth, as decisions are made collectively by the MFO on behalf of multiple families.
• **Lack of scale:** As the SFO is serving only one family, it oftentimes cannot offer the same economies of scale.	• **Potential concerns about confidentiality:** The shared nature of an MFO can leave some families uneasy about whether certain aspects of their family affairs are being shared / discussed within the MFO (even if treated anonymously).
• **Potential for conflict:** An SFO can sometimes lead to conflict within the family, as family members may have differing opinions on how the wealth should be managed. This can be particularly difficult during generational transitions.	• **Lack of control:** Families do not have complete control of resources and information.
• **Continuity / succession:** Relying on a smaller head count, an SFO is more vulnerable to fluctuation (loss of knowledge) and the loss of the principal or a key executive may put continuity at risk.	

It is important to note that the viability of an SFO is dependent on several key factors, including a critical mass of wealth, talent, infrastructure, governance and direct investment opportunities. An SFO needs to have sufficient size to be efficient and effective in managing the family's wealth and assets. Attracting and retaining talent is also crucial, as it is essential to have a skilled and knowledgeable team in place. The SFO's infrastructure needs to be up to the level required to support its operations and decision-making processes. Effective governance is also necessary, as quick and strategic decision-making is essential in today's accelerated and volatile environment. Direct investments offer an interesting opportunity but can also pose a challenge for many SFOs as they require access to opportunities as well as a very specific skillset inside the team. It is important to carefully consider and manage these factors to ensure the success and long-term viability of an SFO.

The Hybrid Family Office

The family-office-as-a-service, or "uberization" of the family office, is a recent phenomenon that draws on the flexibility and benefits of the global, digital economy to develop an ecosystem-style approach to serving the needs of families. This involves a small team, determining what services are core to the family, and deciding what the family will manage in-house and what services and talents can be outsourced or "rented" as required.

Although all the above archetypes have their place and relevance, we see a clear trend in the direction of *hybrid family offices*. This shift is fundamentally reshaping the landscape of family offices. The hybrid family office overcomes some of the key challenges that single family offices face today, as outlined above. We believe this form of family office will continue to gain in popularity. However, it requires the family to have a close grip over their network of service providers to ensure that everything is working towards the same goal. Oftentimes families choose to have a smaller core team in-house that ensures that the family purpose is clear and that all partners and services are aligned with it.

Factors to consider when it comes to choosing the right family office archetype

Setting up a family office is a major (and costly) undertaking. While it is considered a highly desirable goal for many families to set up their own family office, it is important to be aware that there have been cases when the family office did not meet the family's initial expectations. It is, therefore, important to be aware of several factors that you and your family should consider and discuss when it comes to choosing the right family office archetype for your specific situation and needs. Let's go through some of the key factors.

Total family wealth

Costs

Family complexity
(size, geography proximity)

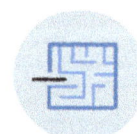

Asset complexity
(assets together, dispersed, liquidity)

Desire / need for customized services

Desire to estabilish a new "hub" for the family
(e.g after a liquidity event)

Confidentiality and risk management

Total family wealth

The right family office archetype is heavily dependent on the overall wealth of a family. Wealthier families may find the SFO archetype to be a viable and sustainable option, while those with less wealth may opt for *virtual* or *hybrid family offices* or *commercial MFOs.*

Determining the minimum investable assets required to establish a successful SFO is a subjective matter. While some experts recommend having at least USD100 million in assets under management, others suggest a higher threshold (in some cases as high as USD 500 million to USD 1 billion). The reason there is no one right answer is that each family is different (as per the assessment in the "Charting your Course" chapter), in terms of size, complexity, needs, etc. Families also vary in terms of their cost sensitivity, meaning that some might be willing to invest a bit more (and in turn diminish their financial returns) to have a worry-free setup, whereas others are more cost sensitive.

Ultimately, it very much depends on the variety of services the family wishes to be handled by their family office (which in turn means an increase in infrastructure, personnel, and so on). SFOs with fewer assets can still achieve effectiveness by focusing on their areas of expertise, limiting their mission and their scope of services, and effectively outsourcing non-core activities.

Recent years have seen an increase in the average size of SFOs. This trend is driven by a need for specialization across asset classes, growing regulatory requirements, and significant upfront infrastructure investment costs. Regardless of size, family offices must tailor their services to meet the specific needs and goals of the family they serve. Ultimately, the success of a family office is measured by its ability to create and preserve wealth for the family over the long term.

Costs

Establishing an SFO incurs both set-up costs, such as infrastructure, office space, and employee expenses, as well as recurring operating costs. The family's ability to sustain these expenses is a critical factor in deciding whether to proceed with setting up an SFO or, instead, go for a predictable, commercial MFO.

The running costs of a family office vary considerably, depending on the size and complexity of your family enterprise ecosystem, the range of service needs that you and your family have, the location you select as costs vary, the types of talents you seek to hire, among other factors. Defining what the "typical" family office cost structure looks like is neither easy nor very useful, simply because no two family offices are alike. However, it is probably fair to say that the annual costs of a single family office will be in the millions, rather than in the hundreds of thousands, of USD. There are a few typical factors to consider when it comes to setup costs and running costs, which we want to briefly illustrate here.

- **Setup costs:** Setting up a family office can be a complex and costly process and can vary from USD 0.5 – 3 million, depending on factors such as the size and complexity of the family as well as the complexity and variety of needs of the family. The setup costs would typically include a variety of expenses such as headhunting services to hire key employees, office space setup and equipment, establishing IT infrastructure, organizing the legal and tax setup and other related costs. To establish an effective family office, it is necessary to invest in the right people, infrastructure, and technology solutions. Therefore, it is important to carefully consider all the cost items involved to ensure that the family office is set up correctly and operates efficiently over the long term.

- **Running costs:** Managing a family office can entail significant annual expenses. These recurring costs typically include personnel-related expenses, such as salaries, bonuses and benefits, as well as expenses related to office rent, IT infrastructure and software maintenance, legal and accounting fees, and other overhead costs. In addition, investment management fees may represent a significant portion of the annual operating expenses, particularly for families with complex and diverse investment portfolios. Depending on the size and complexity of the family office, annual operating costs can range from USD 1 million to several million dollars. Another way to look at it can be in relative terms, with an anecdotal reference point of 80-100 basis points (as a percentage of the assets under management). Although these expenses can be significant, they are necessary to ensure the effective and efficient management of a family's financial affairs and this expenditure can provide a range of benefits, such as greater control over investments, access to specialized expertise and streamlined management of assets.

We will return to the aspect of family office costs (and the financing of these costs) in the "Resources" section later in this chapter.

The complexity of the family enterprise ecosystem

Earlier in the book, during the "Charting your Course" chapter, you had the chance to map out your family enterprise ecosystem, including the various complexities that you have in terms of "who you are," "what you own," "how you function" and "your role in society." As you can imagine, the choice of the right family office archetype largely depends on the complexities that you have in your system.

As family enterprise ecosystems grow in size and complexity, choosing the right family office structure becomes increasingly important. For families with

large, jointly held fortunes and members living worldwide, a single family office may be the only option that adequately meets their needs. However, such an approach can be costly and requires significant resources to manage. In contrast, a multi family office or a *commercial multi family office* may be a more sensible and cost-efficient solution for smaller families with limited needs, such as investment services, estate planning, or simple concierge services. It is crucial to choose the right family office structure that is well-suited to the family's unique situation, taking into account factors such as governance, tax and legal considerations, and the level of control and oversight required.

Desire or need for customized services

Affluent families often require tailored and customized services that meet their unique needs; and they want them to be delivered to them exclusively, without having to "compete" with other families for resources. Depending on the scope and complexity of these customized services, it might be more challenging for multi family offices to take care of them in a fully satisfactory manner. While MFOs can offer economies of scale and provide a broad range of services, the nature of their business means that clients must accept some level of resource-sharing and prioritization with other families. As an MFO serves more families, the services offered become more standardized, and the level of customization may decrease. For instance, managing exceptional projects, such as the startup of a new business or addressing specific legacy issues, may require dedicated resources that a single family office is better suited to provide.

Desire to establish a new hub for the family

Family offices can provide more than just asset management services; they can also serve as a central hub for the family to ensure greater alignment, cohesion, and purpose. While it is key for any family to have such a hub, it is particularly important for families that have been through a major shift or transformation, such as the sale of their legacy business or giving up the operational leadership of their legacy business, whereby the historic "glue" of the family is slowly but surely disappearing.

As families become more complex, the need for a guiding intelligence that understands the family as a whole and how it integrates with its various assets becomes increasingly important. This is where SFOs can excel, providing an integrated approach that adds quality and efficiency to the handling of family affairs. Additionally, SFOs can take on strategic initiatives such as family governance, education coordination, wealth creation and philanthropic activities. While there are many providers catering to wealthy families, those with unique needs may find that a dedicated SFO is the best choice.

Need for confidentiality and risk management

When it comes to choosing the right family office structure, the desire for confidentiality and risk management can be significant factors to consider. Some families may choose to establish an SFO as the best way to limit the number of professionals involved and keep the circulation of information about their private and financial affairs to a minimum. Confidentiality is critical for families, and an SFO can help protect their privacy by centralizing and controlling the flow of information. In addition to this, an SFO can also play a broader role in managing the risks associated with family affairs, including reputational risk. This emphasis on privacy and risk management is essential to the culture of an SFO.

False sense of security

While the desire for confidentiality, privacy and risk management are oftentimes mentioned as key drivers for choosing an SFO, the reality is that family office employees move between family offices and financial institutions – like in any other industry. Therefore, the risk of confidential information leaking out of the SFO is relatively high. Furthermore, SFOs are not necessarily on top of things when it comes to cybersecurity. This can pose significant risks for the family. In contrast, MFOs are mostly regulated and therefore have to meet certain technical and organizational standards, including how to handle sensitive information.

Picking a name

Picking a suitable name for the family office is an important step and must be handled with care. Families are often keen to honor their founders or engage the next generation by naming their organization after certain family members. There are certain advantages and disadvantages to a family's reputation and business if they are closely linked with a family office. Families often want to keep their family office hidden / a secret and, therefore, do not wish to link the name of the company directly to their family name. A few different options to consider:

- Name the family office after the family (Rockefeller Family Office, Walton Enterprises, Soros Family Office)
- Name the family office with abbreviations of family members or places the family is from (for example, Kirkbi, which combines the family name Kirk and the town where LEGO resides, Billund)
- Create a symbolic or family-unrelated name (see Bill Gates' Cascade Investment)

Family office location

While there are several countries and cities around the world that take pride in being major family office hubs, it is advisable to undertake a proper review of various factors that are important to you and your family.

There are several areas to consider when it comes to choosing the location for your family office. Some of these factors are related to you and your family enterprise, others are related to the location's jurisdiction and wealth management ecosystem. Here are some of these factors:

How to select a location?

Family & Lifestyle

- Where does the family live, work and spend leisure time? What is the impact of different geographies and time zone?
- In terms of lifestyle, what are the family's expectations and requirements?
- How will the family maintain control and oversight of the family office?

Ownership Jurisdiction

- What are the relevant legal & tax issues and constraints?
- What is the regulatory environment?
- Does the country offer political and legal stability?
- How likely will there be economic and currency stability in the future?

Wealth Management

- Does this location offer access to markets and investment opportunities?
- Does this location offer access to talent?
- What does the current portfolio look like and where are assets held?
- What is estimated cost of running a family office in this location?

FAMILY OFFICE CLOSE TO HOME	←●●●●●●●●●● →	FAMILY OFFICE IN A MAJOR FO HUB

Having the family office close to where you and your family are located

Having the family office located in one of the world's major family office hubs

Evidently, major family office hubs in the US, Europe and Asia tick many of the boxes regarding the framework conditions that are critical for the success of a family office. However, you and your family will need to carefully reflect on how important it is for you to have the family office close to you versus the benefits of being exposed to these family office hotspots or whether privacy is a key factor for you, so that you might prefer a more rural setup as opposed to a major family office city. The decision is largely dependent on your family enterprise ecosystem, your specific needs and the overall purpose and focus of your family office. For instance, if you wish your family office to serve as a new hub for your family because you sold your legacy business, then it might make more sense to locate the family office close to your home. However, if the primary or sole purpose of your family office is to manage your family's wealth by being exposed to the best investment deals, then it makes a lot of sense that the family office be based in the market where you wish to make your investments or where you have the best possible framework conditions for doing business.

A recent trend has been that families choose more than one location for their family office, with one office serving as the central hub for the family and other offices in close proximity to family members around the world or close to key investments or investment opportunities.

In conclusion, you and your family must carefully consider your long-term strategic goals when making decisions about the location of your family office. We recommend that you work through this step with advisors who know and understand both the specific requirements of a family office and the specificities of different locations. We will get to this point in Activity 2 at the end of this section.

ACTIVITIES

The following two activities will help you and your family answer fundamental questions related to the structure and setup of your family office. Keep in mind that the family office you decide to set up should reflect your family enterprise ecosystem and your family manifesto, help you bring to life your desired family office purpose and cater to your specific needs. Hence, we recommend going through the following activities while having your answers to the *Navigator's* previous activities at hand.

> **Family Office Navigator questions:**
>
> - What type of family office do we wish to establish and where?
> - How will we go about setting it up?

ACTIVITY 1:
SELECTING YOUR FAMILY OFFICE ARCHETYPE

Now that we have discussed the different factors that can help you select the optimal family office structure, we invite you to go through each of these dimensions and reflect on where you sit in each spectrum.

Step 1:
Map out the factors influencing your family office structure

Individually, complete the following table and indicate where you and your family sit on each of the dimensions listed, from low (left) to high (right).

LOW	1	2	3	4	5	HIGH

< 30 million USD	**TOTAL FINANCIAL WEALTH** Overall financial wealth of you or your family 1　2　3　4　5	> 500 million USD
30-50 basis points (bps)	**COSTS** Willingness or ability to handle costs associated with the family office 1　2　3　4　5	100+ basis points (bps)
Small family, concentrated in one location, G1 or G2, concentrated assets	**COMPLEXITY OF THE FAMILY ENTERPRISE ECOSYSTEM** How large and complex is your family enterprise ecosystem? 1　2　3　4　5	Large, complex and globally scattered family of multiple generations, diversified assets and multiple business & investment activities
No real need for customized services	**DESIRE / NEED FOR CUSTOMIZED SERVICES** 1　2　3　4　5	The family expects many different customized services

No real need for a new family hub. The family already has strong unifying forces	DESIRE / NEED FOR A NEW FAMILY HUB (for example, after selling the legacy business, letting go of operational control or shifting the geographic focus of the family) 1 2 3 4 5	There is a strong need for a new hub for the family to ensure unity and togetherness
No particular need for confidentiality	DESIRE / NEED FOR CONFIDENTIALITY 1 2 3 4 5	Strong confidentiality requirements
No particular need for concentrated risk management	DESIRE / NEED FOR RISK MANAGEMENT 1 2 3 4 5	Strong need for concentrated risk management

Note: Inspired by the UBS Family Office Compass

Step 2:
Compare answers within your family group

In your family group, review your different responses to the dimensions featured in Step 1. Compare and discuss your answers in case there are any major differences.

Step 3:
Define your preferred structure

Reflect on your collective answers and what these might mean for your family office structure of the future. In general, the further to the right you are in your answers, the more likely it is that you will wish to set up an SFO in order to cater to your specific needs and complexities.

ACTIVITY 2:
FAMILY OFFICE LOCATION

Let's revisit the different dimensions that we introduced earlier in the chapter with respect to the choice of location for the family office. We now encourage you to go deeper in your analysis of the right location, including an in-depth due diligence. This activity serves solely as a basis to get the discussion going and to help you narrow your search field.

Step 1:
Map out the family-specific factors influencing the choice of location for your family office

Go through the following table and indicate where you and your family sit on each of the dimensions listed. You might want to revisit your answers to Activity 1 to help you complete this activity.

	Strongly disagree				Strongly agree
	1	2	3	4	5
Family office as hub The family office is meant to serve as a hub for our family to foster communication and togetherness and therefore we wish to have the family office close to us.	1	2	3	4	5
Family office involved with non-financial affairs The family office will play a major role in helping our family manage the full variety of total family wealth, including human capital, social capital, financial capital, reputational capital, intellectual capital, and so on.	1	2	3	4	5

Family control of the family office Our family will be closely involved in the operations or governance oversight of the family office.	1 2 3 4 5
Family assets We hold most of our assets in one location / country.	1 2 3 4 5
Family office ecosystem It is important to us that the family office is located in one of the major family office hubs of the world.	1 2 3 4 5
Access to talent It is important to us that the family has access to highly qualified, specialized (and affordable) staff for the family office.	1 2 3 4 5

Step 2:
Shortlist of possible locations

Create a shortlist of potential locations for your family office. This should probably include locations that are close to you and your family as well as some selected strategic locations so that you can compare these locations based on the various dimensions we have discussed. We suggest that you focus on 2-3 different locations at this stage.

Step 3:
Desk research

How do the shortlisted locations measure against the following dimensions? It might be helpful to consult other sources of information about these countries / regions, such as the IMD World Competitiveness Ranking.

In the following table, rank these locations on a range of dimensions, ranging from 1 (low / not favorable for a family office) to 5 (high / very favorable for a family office).

In order to complete this table, you will want to do some desk research, and it is advisable to also consult experts who understand the various family office needs and understand the specific contextual factors for each of these locations. You might also want to reach out to some of the regional promotion agencies in the locations you are focusing on, as well as other families you might know (or might be able to be introduced to) to understand their assessment of each location.

This will then serve as a basis for your ultimate decision on where you and your family will want to set up the family office. It is not necessarily something you have to decide right now, but it is an important decision to agree on in the near future, once you have completed the navigator journey.

	Location Rate from 1 (low / unfavorable) to 5 (high / very favorable)		
	LOCATION 1	LOCATION 2	LOCATION 3

FAMILY FACTORS

	LOCATION 1	LOCATION 2	LOCATION 3
Proximity to family members			
Proximity to key assets or activities of the family			
Alignment of location with family's long-term goals (diversification, risks, succession, future location shifts, etc.)			
Privacy			
Cost of living			
Quality of life			

ACCESS TO EXPERTS

	LOCATION 1	LOCATION 2	LOCATION 3
Access to investment opportunities			
Access to talents and experts			
Costs of running the family office			
Access to key service providers (lawyers, accountants, investment managers)			

FRAMEWORK CONDITIONS OF THE MARKET

	LOCATION 1	LOCATION 2	LOCATION 3
Ease of setting up a business			
Legal system			
Regulatory system			
Tax system			
Business environment			
Political and legal stability			
Infrastructure			
Economic stability			
Currency stability			
Costs of running the family office			

OTHER FACTORS

	LOCATION 1	LOCATION 2	LOCATION 3

RESOURCES

Setting the scene

When we talk about the resources of the family office, we are referring to factors such as:

- your family office talent (human resources)
- the partners you choose for your family office journey (your social resources)
- the financing of your family office activities (financial resources)

In short, assembling the right resources is essential to set up and operate the family office, as well as to manage administrative aspects such as infrastructure and the back office. In this section, we will provide an overview of key resources and discuss points that are worth considering as you work out what you need for your family office to function effectively.

Family office talents – human resources

Hiring the right talent into the family office is probably the most important step because the job of a family officer is a highly personal one. This is especially true since many family offices operate in a relatively lean manner, relying on the qualities of a few key employees. Mobilizing the best human resources for the family office means finding the right kind of talents for your family and its ecosystem.

The family office will likely engage both family and non-family talents in various functions of operations and oversight. It is important for families to determine which role they can and should play in the context of the family office, including the extent of any involvement in day-to-day operations and decision-making.

More broadly, the scope of the family office staff will vary considerably depending on the complexity of the family enterprise ecosystem, the purpose and needs of the family and the types of services you wish your family office to focus on.

In this section, we will focus on the following questions:

- What are the overall functions and roles to be fulfilled in the family office and what are the key responsibilities of each role?
- What skills and competencies will you look for when hiring non-family members for the family office and how can you evaluate these qualities during the hiring process?
- How should compensation for family office executives be structured and what factors should be taken into consideration when determining the appropriate levels of compensation?
- Which roles can or should family members play in the family office and what are the potential benefits and drawbacks of having family members in certain positions?

Roles and responsibilities within the family office

To ensure the efficient functioning of a family office, a diverse range of roles and responsibilities is required that involves both family and non-family members. We will briefly describe the key roles that you would typically find in a family office.

In reality, many of these roles will be combined, especially in the earlier phases of a family office or in smaller family offices. However, it is helpful to understand the different functional roles and responsibilities within a family office. For example, it is not unusual to see combined roles, such as the CEO and CIO, or the CFO and COO. Also, for very hands-on principals, it is not uncommon that they take the operational lead of the family office in the beginning.

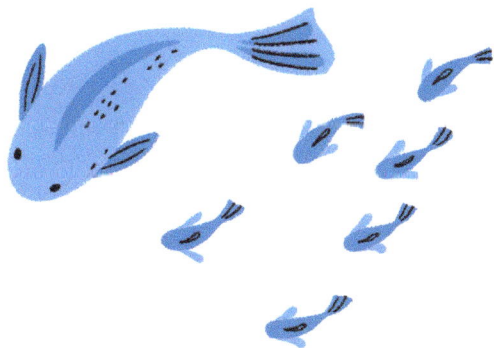

ROLE	DESCRIPTION
Principal	The role of the principal in a family office is crucial as they are the owners of the family office and it is up to them to decide who makes the decisions. The principal can choose to be involved in the day-to-day operations or take a more hands-off approach. They can take on the role of President / CEO or non-executive or executive director. Regardless of the title, the principal needs to be clear about their wants and needs for the family office. Their involvement or lack thereof can impact the staff and tone of the office, with greater emphasis placed on financial reporting and more responsibility delegated to investment executives if the principal chooses to take a more hands-off approach.
President / CEO / Head of the Family Office	This is the most senior position in the family office. The president / CEO is responsible for overall direction and strategy and is accountable to the board of directors, which typically includes family owners, investment professionals and non-family wealth experts. The president / CEO must balance short-term goals with a long-range view of the family's wealth and multigenerational objectives, while serving as the primary representative of the family.

In many cases (especially in the early phase of the family office), this role will be handled by a family member – a dynamic, hands-on wealth creator or 2nd or 3rd generation wealth owner who has the necessary influence and connections within the family to engage the wider family group to participate in the family office project, together.

This role calls for a versatile change agent who can help the family ensure continuity while also anticipating necessary changes to keep the office evolving. The ideal candidate will have extensive experience in general management, business management and people management, with specific knowledge of wealth management, tax, investments, foundations and philanthropy, trust and estate planning, as well as risk management. Additionally, strong leadership, communication, and execution skills are essential. |
| **Chief Investment Officer (CIO)** | The CIO develops and executes investment strategies that align with the family's objectives, staying up to date with markets, identifying opportunities, and managing portfolios of private and public equities. The CIO provides risk management, communication of investment performance data, and maintains relationships with external wealth managers to ensure compliance with relevant policies and procedures. The CIO advises the family based on predefined policies, participates in family council sessions and updates the investment committee / board regularly.

Under the CIO you will typically find a range of specialists that help execute the investment strategy, depending on the set up and strategy in play. This could involve investment managers, portfolio managers or investment analysts. |

Chief Financial Officer (CFO)	The CFO oversees the office's financial functions and ensures compliance with regulatory and reporting requirements. The CFO formulates financial policies and plans, provides direction for tax, insurance, budget, credit, and treasury functions, and manages financial transactions, policies, and procedures to meet the family office's short- and long-term objectives.
	The CFO also oversees the family members' personal tax issues, coordinates with legal counsel and the CIO and communicates vital financial information to family members and key stakeholders. In addition to financial management, the CFO may assist in evaluating business and real estate opportunities and act as the family's primary risk officer.
Chief Operations Officer (COO)	The COO is responsible for overseeing the day-to-day operations of the organization. This includes managing staff, ensuring compliance with legal and regulatory requirements, and implementing operational strategies. Depending on the scale and complexity of the family office, the COO may take on a variety of roles, from overseeing IT and security to managing front- and back-office operations. In addition, the COO is also focused on data management and mitigating operational risks and works closely with other executives and family members to provide guidance and support, ensuring that the family office is meeting the needs of its clients and stakeholders.

Skills and competencies of family officers

Families often start the recruiting process through their personal and professional network. Besides technical skills and experiences in the domains of finance, law and accounting, among others, the overall family fit is essential. A family officer must demonstrate trustworthiness, integrity, flexibility and discretion, along with other soft skills. Evidently, you want to ensure that anyone you onboard is among the best in their field and will bring with them the necessary hard skills, but those traits alone will not necessarily produce the results that you might be looking for. You will want to ensure that your family officers combine the right professional competence with the right level of "family fit" and trust, which is difficult to find.

In a family office, every staff member is responsible for fulfilling their own technical role, such as managing investments, handling a real estate portfolio, administering a portfolio of private equity investments, setting up family education programs or family events, overseeing operations, and so forth. The tangible skills needed for each role will vary greatly in different family offices and from one expert to another, according to the scope of services and activities that the family office offers.

There are also several intangible responsibilities that employees must be capable of handling, which relate to family dynamics. Let's now focus on some of those intangible skills and capabilities, which we believe are essential for the success of any family office executive.

SKILL & EXPERIENCE	DESCRIPTION
Previous experience with family offices vs. your specific family	While previous experience in a family office can be beneficial, arguably the most important factor is previous experience working with an owning family – rather than just general experience working with other families. Additionally, positions within a family office should normally be based on professional merit rather than family connections.
Stewardship	As a family officer, it is essential to adopt a stewardship mindset to effectively manage and protect the family's assets for the long-term. While a fiduciary mindset focuses on managing assets according to legal and ethical obligations, a stewardship mindset goes beyond this to consider the impact of decisions on future generations and the broader community: preserving and enhancing the family's wealth while also considering the social and environmental implications of investment decisions. By adopting a stewardship mindset, family officers can ensure that they are acting in the best interests of the family while also contributing positively to society. This approach can also help to build trust and foster a sense of responsibility and accountability within the family, ensuring the long-term success of the family enterprise.
Emotional intelligence (EQ)	Family officers require a high level of EQ due to the emotional nature of the working culture. In smaller family offices, where rules are less clearly articulated, decisions often must be made based on the idiosyncratic emotional landscape of a given day. Family officers need to be skilled in dealing with family tensions that can leak into even the most technical financial conversations. They should have some formal family systems training, which will help them understand the psychology of family dynamics and deal with complex situations. In larger family offices, there may be specialized teams that pull together in a structure like a business or corporation, but in smaller offices, the absence of established rules makes a high EQ essential.
Trustworthiness	The trustworthiness of family office executives is crucial to their success, as a lack of trust can result in wasted time and the need to find replacements. Trust takes time to build, and when recruiting, it is important to look for candidates with both the ability to get the job done and moral uprightness. Aligned values are also an important characteristic and can make the difference between success and failure when the pressure is on. Discretion and loyalty are paramount for family office executives as they can be called on for help at any time.

Humility and respect	Another critical skill is the ability to demonstrate humility and respect towards the family they serve. Humility allows a family officer to operate without ego and to accept decisions made by the family, even if it does not align with their own opinions or suggestions. This is essential for building trust and rapport with family members and stakeholders and maintaining positive relationships. By demonstrating respect towards the family's values, traditions, and objectives, the family officer can effectively support the family in achieving their goals.
Hard-working diplomatic rebel	An effective family officer is a hard-working "diplomatic rebel." While humility and a laid-back approach are important, family officers must be prepared for long hours of desk work. In most cases, the head of the family in a family office is a serial entrepreneur who has spent 30 to 40 years building a business from the ground up and sold it for hundreds of millions. Family office executives must, therefore, be able to cope with the entrepreneur's alpha personality and the 10 to 20 ideas they generate every day. Family officers must have strength of character and the ability to speak truth to power because family offices lack the checks and balances found in the corporate world. Succession planning is also important, and family office executives must have an independent mindset, be respectful, and yet independent of their principal. By being a hard-working diplomatic rebel, family officers can strike the right balance between what the principal wants and what they need to ensure overall success.

Beware the lonely banker

A common - and quite logical - approach for families is to ask their trusted banker if he or she is interested in joining them in their family office. So far, they have been very happy with their performance. So why not have them 100% devoted to their specific investment wishes and needs? Sounds great on paper, but it is important to keep in mind that the performance of an investment expert is, in part, driven by the network they are embedded in. While they are inside the bank, they have access to analytics, tools, databases and professional networks. As soon as you take them out of this environment, you essentially cut (or hamper) their connection to some of the factors that have been driving your portfolio's performance. Hence, it will require a rethinking on your and their side when it comes to areas such as scouting for and assessing deals, analyzing and benchmarking investment managers.

Compensation of family office executives

The compensation of executives in a family office can vary considerably depending on the size and complexity of the organization, as well as the specific roles and responsibilities of each executive. In general, executive compensation in family offices tends to be structured differently than in traditional corporate environments, as the primary objective is often to preserve wealth and ensure long-term stability, rather than maximize short-term profits.

The inconvenient truth about family offices is that they are in direct competition with other players in the financial industry and, while family offices are largely structured as cost centers, they compete with other profit-generating and mostly larger players that can offer more in terms of total compensation and more varied career options.

To attract and retain top talent, family offices can offer a combination of fixed salaries, performance-based annual bonuses / incentives and long-term incentive plans (LTI). However, the specific compensation structure and levels may also be influenced by the family's personal values and philosophy, as well as their overall approach to wealth management. In the following table, we will elaborate on the different compensation and incentive structures.

TYPE OF COMPENSATION	DESCRIPTION
Base salary	The base salary should be positioned in a range that is comparable with what they would receive elsewhere in their profession (in the financial, advisory, legal or tax industry, for instance). Some family offices choose to pay slightly above the industry averages to compensate for a lack of career advancement options in a family office. However, before paying a disproportionately larger base salary, it can make sense to think more broadly and play with different types of incentive mechanisms that traditional industry players cannot really work with, such as specific long-term incentive plans (as outlined below).
Annual incentive plan	An annual incentive plan is a structured compensation scheme that is determined at the beginning of the year, whereby the principal and the executive agree on specific objectives for the year. The incentive plan may incorporate both financial and non-financial performance measures, and it aims to create alignment with the family's strategic vision across various goals.
Discretionary bonus	A discretionary bonus is a type of bonus that is not determined by a specific formula or performance metrics. Instead, it is determined at the discretion of the family office's leadership or board of directors, based on various factors such as individual performance, contribution to the success of the organization and overall economic performance of the office. This type of bonus is typically set and granted on an end-of-year annual basis and is not guaranteed.
Non-cash benefits	Non-cash benefits are important to attract, motivate, and retain talent. Generous packages with benefits like pensions, medical insurance and cars, along with a good work-life balance, are attractive to employees. Additionally, some may value the chance to work in a less mainstream corporate environment and be loyal to family owners they identify with.
Long-term incentive (LTI) plan	Long-term incentive (LTI) plans and participation models with deferred compensation are increasingly being used by family offices to incentivize their executives. These plans aim to motivate and retain top talent by providing them with equity or other forms of ownership in the family office or its underlying investments. Participation models allow executives to share in the growth and value creation of the family office over the long term. This aligns their interests with those of the family and encourages them to stay with the organization for an extended period. In some examples, the compensation is deferred with a vesting period of several years, thus ensuring the long-term alignment of employee interests with those of the family.

Examples of long-term incentive (LTI) plans

Family offices can offer a variety of LTI plans, with the ultimate goal of increasing executives' long-term commitment and participation:

Equity-based plans	Equity-based plans are a type of long-term incentive plan that grants ownership or equity interests in the family office or the family's operating businesses to executives. The most common types of equity-based plans include stock options, restricted stock units (RSUs) and phantom stock. Stock awards or other company equity are a popular form of equity-based plans that grant actual shares of the company to executives. Phantom or synthetic equity, on the other hand, is a stock equivalent that provides some of the benefits of stock ownership and is sometimes referred to as shadow stock. These types of plans are mostly used by family offices that have strong management and / or oversight of the family operating company or companies.
Carried interest / phantom carry	Carried interest or phantom carry is a type of long-term incentive plan that is commonly used in the private equity and hedge fund industries. This plan provides a share of the profits earned from investments made by the fund or firm over a certain period. The executive is typically required to hold the investment for a set period to align their interests with those of the fund or firm's investors. Phantom carry, also known as synthetic carry, is a similar plan that provides a similar share of profits, but without actual ownership of the investments. This type of incentive plan is designed to encourage executives to make profitable investments and hold them for the long term, as their compensation is tied to the success of the fund or firm.
Deferred compensation plans	Family office executives often receive deferred compensation based on performance metrics tied to long-term goals. This aligns their interests with those of the family and encourages sustainable decisions that benefit the family. This mechanism is commonly used alongside non-qualified deferred compensation plans to aid in tax planning. Long-term incentive plans can include immediate cash payouts with portions vesting in a few years, or even extreme forms such as employee benefit trusts. Deferred compensation incentivizes risk management, interest alignment and clawback opportunities.

Co-investment opportunities	Co-investment opportunities allow executives to invest alongside the family, providing access to exclusive deals that would otherwise be unavailable. However, families must carefully consider their objectives - as well as their tax, and legal position - before entering these arrangements. Co-investments are most commonly used by families with in-house public and private investment teams. To finance these investments, leverage is often incorporated into the plan. Families can provide leverage through recourse loans that charge an interest rate and are repaid from transaction proceeds and / or plan vesting. Alternatively, non-recourse loans may be offered, which do not require repayment. On the downside, such co-investments present a possible source of conflict of interest. An executive may direct most attention to investments where he / she has "skin in the game" and pay less attention to other parts of the portfolio. Also, co-investment opportunities may bias the selection / due diligence process towards investments the co-investing executive may have a personal preference for.

Aligning LTIs with the risk associated with certain investments

When thinking about LTIs for family office management, it is important to keep in mind what level of risk is associated with which types of investments and how the managements' LTIs are linked to this risk. The reality is that families do not always fully understand the long-term implications of certain wealth strategies, which could invite CIOs or investment teams to take more risk than is appropriate, simply with the goal of maximizing their long-term plans, while reducing their personal risk. It is important to manage this aspect carefully with an independent, outside partner who can help you establish and set up the LTIs.

Succession planning for family officers

Establishing robust succession plans for key employees and family officers within family offices is of paramount importance. These individuals often hold a wealth of tacit knowledge accumulated over years of experience, meaning their departure or sudden absence poses a significant risk to the continuity and effectiveness of the family office's operations. This is, of course, no different from any key function in a business, but due to the specific nature of family offices, the risk is more pronounced. Proper succession planning mitigates this risk by identifying and grooming potential successors, ensuring a smooth transition in case of departure, illness, or death.

Additionally, when a generational transition takes place within the family, careful consideration is required. While experienced family officers who have served the parents possess valuable insights and have developed trusting relationships, the evolving dynamics of the younger generation's goals and preferences might necessitate a generational shift in the leadership team. Balancing continuity with fresh perspectives becomes crucial to stewarding the family's wealth across generations. Here is an overview of the pros and cons of keeping the existing family office management intact versus introducing new management during the generational transition.

Keeping the old management intact	Introducing new management
• **Continuity of relationships and knowledge:** Family officers who have served the parents have likely developed strong relationships and an in-depth understanding of the family's history, values, and unique preferences. This historical knowledge can be critical in managing family dynamics, investments and other affairs. • **Stability and trust:** Transitioning to a new leadership team can cause disruption and uncertainty. Maintaining familiar faces at the helm can provide a sense of stability and continuity, fostering trust among family members and stakeholders. • **Preservation of legacy:** Family officers who have worked closely with the previous generation can help preserve the family's legacy and ensure that the principles and strategies upheld by the parents are effectively carried forward.	• **Fresh perspectives:** A new leadership team brings fresh ideas, perspectives, and insights. They can introduce innovative strategies, technologies, and approaches that align with the changing times. • **Alignment with the next generation:** The new leadership team can better understand and cater to the needs, preferences and aspirations of the younger generation, facilitating a smoother intergenerational wealth transfer. • **Adaptability:** A new team is likely to be more adaptable to evolving market conditions and industry trends, enabling the family office to stay competitive and seize new opportunities. Ideally, they are hired after the next generation has developed their own strategic plans and priorities for the family office to ensure that they have the necessary skills and capabilities to execute that strategy.
• **Resistance to change:** Long-standing family officers might be resistant to adopting new strategies, technologies, or approaches that the younger generation wishes to implement, potentially hindering innovation and growth. • **Generation gap:** The evolving goals, aspirations, and preferences of the younger generation might not align with those of the previous one. Family officers from the older generation may struggle to understand and cater to the needs of the new generation. It can also hinder the next generation from really taking charge of matters. • **Stagnation:** Sticking with the same leadership team could result in complacency and a lack of fresh perspectives. This can hinder adaptability to new market trends and shifts in the economic landscape.	• **Loss of institutional knowledge:** Transitioning to a new leadership team may lead to a loss of historical knowledge and relationships that the older family officers possessed. This could potentially impact decision-making and family dynamics. • **Trust building:** Establishing trust with a new leadership team takes time. Family members and stakeholders may need to adapt to new personalities and strategies, potentially causing initial uncertainties. • **Cultural alignment:** A new leadership team may take time to fully align with the family's values and traditions, potentially leading to clashes of culture and vision.

Involvement of family members in the family office

Family involvement in the family office is a key topic that families need to think about. It will vary from family to family depending on several factors: the family's stage of development and overall complexity, the range of services the family expects and whether there are any family members with the necessary skills and interest to hold a position in the family office. A first-generation wealth creator will most likely be hands-on in the creation and operation of the family office – as family office president and sometimes even CEO, depending on his or her skills in wealth management. In more advanced and complex family systems, the overall family office staff will more likely be non-family, while family members sit in the overarching governance bodies for oversight and control.

Like in any family business, there is the risk of conflict between siblings, cousins, generations or branches when it comes to specific family hiring decisions, especially when the overall performance is not what was expected by the wider family or if the overall risk profile is markedly different between family members.

It is important that families define family employment policies that clarify potential roles and required qualifications for participation in the family office. Furthermore, it is advisable to clarify if family members should play an operational role in the family office or remain at the governance / oversight level.

Choosing your partners – your social resources

In the world of family offices, it's often necessary to seek external partners to achieve your goals in managing family wealth. These partners can bring valuable expertise, resources, and guidance, filling gaps in the family's capabilities. These partners may include board members, investment managers, advisors and service providers. Partnering with external experts and organizations is crucial for success in managing family wealth. However, selecting the right partners is a delicate process that requires careful consideration of the family's needs, objectives and desired level of professionalism.

In this section, we will elaborate on some of the most common types of partners that you and your family and family office should consider for your activities.

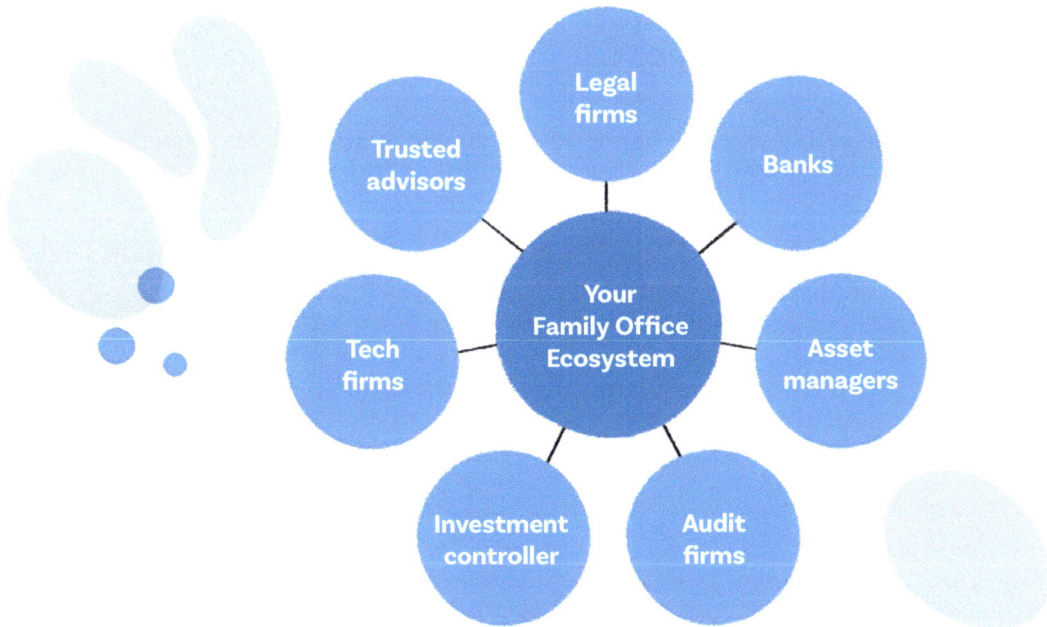

For legal support, a high-quality law firm is essential to provide advice on various aspects, including structuring, contracts, tax and estate planning. It's important to ensure that the law firm can advise across different jurisdictions and areas of activity.

Investment banks and private banks play a central role in developing the family business and family office. They offer access to finance, global custody, consolidated reporting, analytics, direct trading and research. Banks can also provide off-the-shelf IT investment tools and assist with sourcing deals, financing, corporate finance and executing transactions. A family office typically works with one to six banks, each performing specific roles that match their strengths.

Asset managers provide expertise in specific asset classes. Most family offices prefer outsourcing tactical allocation and instrument selection to various specialist firms rather than relying solely on one counterparty. A family office typically works with five to ten asset managers.

Accounting firms can support family offices when they are setting up, hiring key people, and during times of pressure or crisis. They provide financial accounting expertise and may offer internal accounting capabilities when needed.

Not all family offices arrange external audits, but many value them for objective scrutiny and advice on establishing adequate financial controls. This is especially valuable when the family's ownership is complex, with varying interests, involvement and financial knowledge.

What we see increasingly in the most professional family offices is that they engage an Investment Controller who, unlike an auditor, examines the Investment Policy Statement (IPS) and evaluates how well investments comply with the IPS (asset allocation ranges, concentration risks, risk budget, liquidity, etc.). The Investment Controller also compares performance on a risk-adjusted basis with the performance of markets and the performance of competing investment managers. This function typically reports directly to the Investment Committee or the Chairman of the Board to ensure transparency with the family. This is a critical function for families in which not all asset owners are represented in the governance bodies, if only selected family members operate the family office, or if different family members have vastly different levels of financial literacy. An investment controller offers asset owners peace of mind that their interests are protected and that family office activities are aligned with their overarching objectives.

Good IT support is essential, and it may be necessary to engage external providers who can supply highly specialized IT solutions. Even if the family office decides to build internal capabilities, external providers can still help with specialized and new IT solutions. Financial reporting and cybersecurity are two of many key IT-related jobs in the context of family offices. While there are many tools available in the market, it is essential to conduct a due diligence on the different tools and see if they match the family's needs. The cost of switching between providers is high, so a proper due diligence at the beginning of the process can save a lot of time and money.

Finally, engaging family advisors can be beneficial in various spheres, from creating a family office to aligning family vision and family governance, as well as developing and integrating the next generation. Advisors can also foster learning and best practice sharing through peer exchange networks and platforms.

The principal-agent problem

When families amass significant wealth, ensuring its effective management and growth can be challenging. When these families delegate the management of their wealth to external agents, such as financial advisors, fund managers or wealth management firms, they face several issues. These issues spring mainly from the principal-agent problem. The principal-agent problem arises when one party (the agent) is supposed to act in the best interests of another party (the principal), but their interests don't perfectly align, leading to potential conflicts.

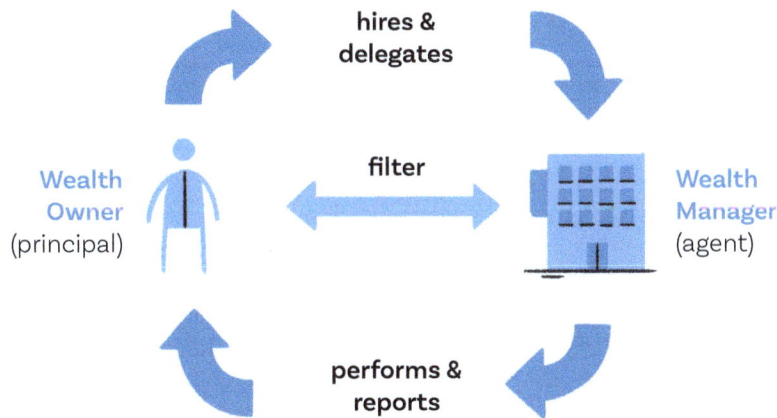

1. **Misaligned incentives:** This is the crux of the principal-agent problem. Financial advisors or wealth managers are often compensated based on the volume of transactions or the assets they manage. This might incentivize them to recommend transactions more frequently (churning) or encourage clients to invest in particular products that provide the managers with higher commissions, even if these aren't the best choices for the family's financial goals.

2. **Information asymmetry:** Agents typically have more knowledge about financial markets, products and strategies than the families (principals). The knowledge gap can make it difficult for the family to ascertain whether the agent is acting in their best interest. Agents might utilize complex financial jargon or recommend sophisticated strategies that the family doesn't fully understand, making the principal dependent on the agent's recommendations, even if they aren't optimal.

3. **Monitoring costs:** Even if a family is aware of potential misaligned incentives, effectively monitoring an agent can be time-consuming and costly. This can include understanding the investment choices, tracking performance, evaluating fees and ensuring that the strategies align with the family's goals and risk tolerance. If the costs of monitoring are too high, it may deter the family from doing so effectively.

4. **Loss of control and confidentiality:** Delegating wealth management means sharing sensitive financial information with external parties. This can lead to concerns about data security, privacy, and potential misuse of confidential information.

5. **Contractual challenges:** The terms of engagement with financial managers or advisors often involve contracts. Ensuring that these contracts are fair, transparent and protective of the family's interests can be a challenge. For instance, contracts might have clauses that shield agents from certain liabilities, making it difficult for the principal to seek redress in cases of mismanagement.

Mapping out your Request for Proposals (RFP) process for choosing the right partners

1. **Identify your needs**: Ideally, the family starts with an Investment Policy Statement (IPS) to sketch out where they want to go and what they want to achieve. The IPS is like a flight plan for the family office. This will help any service provider scale and scope its offer.
2. **Determine the areas where you require external support and services:** These may include legal, financial, IT, accounting, asset management and other related areas.
3. **Define your criteria:** Develop a set of criteria that the partners must meet, including their experience, qualifications, skills, reputation and pricing. Also, consider their compatibility with your family office's values, culture, and goals.
4. **Draft the RFP document:** Prepare a clear and concise RFP document that outlines your needs, criteria and expectations for partners. It should also include instructions on how to submit the proposal, deadlines and contact information.
5. **Identify potential partners:** Research and identify potential partners that meet your criteria. Consider factors such as their track record, experience, reputation and compatibility with your family office.
6. **Send the RFP:** Send the RFP to potential partners and provide them with a deadline to submit their proposals.
7. **Evaluate the proposals:** Review and evaluate the proposals received based on your criteria. Consider their suitability, experience, qualifications and pricing.
8. **Shortlist potential partners:** Shortlist the partners that meet your criteria and schedule a meeting or call to discuss their proposals and address any questions or concerns.
9. **Conduct due diligence:** Conduct due diligence on the shortlisted partners, including reviewing their references, credentials and reputation.
10. **Decide on your partners:** Based on the evaluation and due diligence, decide on the partner or partners that best meet your needs.
11. **Negotiate and finalize the agreement:** Negotiate the terms of the agreement with the selected partner and finalize the agreement once both parties are satisfied.

Financing your family office activities – your financial resources

A critical question to address in your family office journey is: Who pays for what? This is both relevant for the initial setup of the family office as well as its future operations. Setting up a family office is, in principle, similar to the launch of any other new venture activity. The main difference, however, is that the cost of setting up and operating a family office is, typically, significantly higher than in the case of a startup.

Typical cost items to consider in the setup and operational phase of your family office are:

- Personnel (salaries, bonuses, incentives, social cost)
- Headhunter fees to search for key functions
- Office (rent, services, furnishing, deposits, refurbishing)
- IT infrastructure (hardware, software, maintenance, connectivity, servers, security)
- Legal, tax and audit
- Travel and representation expenses
- Administration fees
- Insurances
- In case your family office is an MFO, you also need to consider expenses related to the promotion of your family office through marketing and sales activities.

Setup costs can vary widely and can range from a few hundred thousand USD to a million, depending on a variety of factors such as:

- Complexity and variety of the scope and mandate of the family office
- Need for a headhunter to recruit professionals
- Cost structure of the location of the family office (country, city, location in the city, cost of talent, cost of services, etc.)
- Desire for an office space that matches the family's preferences (look and feel inside the family office)

The initial capital for the setup of the family office can either take the form of an equity investment, a loan that is later repaid or a mix of both. How this is provided by the family is dependent on a series of factors, including the number of family members to be supported by the family office, whether (part of the) wealth is held together (e.g., in a holding company) or individually by each family member and whether everyone from the family participates in the family office or just a few individuals.

The easiest scenario, of course, is when there is only one principal wealth owner (patriarch or matriarch) who decides to set up a family office. In that case he or she covers the whole cost and is the sole owner, until the next generation comes into the picture. It becomes slightly more complex in the case of a larger family with mixed wealth structures and / or different levels of interest and needs with respect to the family office. If there is an existing, shared holding entity, the initial family office costs are often covered by the joint entity. If such a shared holding does not exist or the family office is an initiative of only a few family members, it might be more appropriate for those family members to join forces and finance the initial setup from their personal wealth, likely with some sort of equity stake or partnership model.

Another critical question that families need to answer relates to the fees and costs charged to any clients of the family office. In simpler structures with one principal owner, this is no issue, of course, but it starts to require a structured reflection as soon as there are two or more family members involved who each might have different needs and requirements from the family office. Here are a few different approaches for charging clients of the family office:

- **Hourly rates:** This fee structure is a simple, accurate, and transparent model where the family office charges a standard hourly rate for the service provided to the family client. This rate is communicated openly upfront and depends on the role and seniority of the employee or service provider. This model can be beneficial for services that you might not need on a regular basis or when you have large differences in "usage" of that service by different family members / households.
- **Fixed service fee:** The family office charges a fixed, annual fee to the client, which is calculated based on the family's assets and needs. This approach has the advantage of plannability but has the disadvantage that it might not always be fully clear how much is really needed at the beginning of the year, which can result in overspending. It requires a regular review of the fee structure so that it remains accurate and acceptable. For many families, this often becomes the standard approach.
- **Percentage of AUM:** Family office fees can be charged as a percentage of the assets under management (AUM). This is a relatively common model, especially for the investment services of MFOs. Typically, the fees decrease with an increasing amount of assets, with a minimum fee being charged regardless of the assets.

A key question to address when it comes to the cost structure of a family office is whether it is intended to operate as a profitable entity or whether it should operate on a break-even basis and, as such, optimize the cost structure for family clients. The break-even model is mostly adopted when a family fully owns the family office (SFO), whereas the profit approach tends to be more suitable if the family decides to offer employees an ownership stake as part of a profit-sharing incentive.

Legal structure and ownership of the family office

When it comes to deciding on the legal and ownership structure for your family office, you need to take into consideration several aspects to ensure that you do not make any mistakes later in the process. Often, the family office starts in an informal way, embedded within an operating business. The affairs of the family are dealt with by trusted key employees of the business. While this brings with it structural simplicity and convenience in the early phase, it can become impractical or even create legal conflicts at a later stage. In several cases, families told us that they switched to a more formal structure after they had an IPO and needed to separate their personal and business affairs. It also makes sense for families to separate their different types of assets, in particular their liability-prone assets in operating businesses, from the rest of their family assets.

In principle, ownership must be separated with respect to legal ownership and beneficial ownership. The way in which ownership is compartmentalized depends on the legal and tax jurisdiction, the family enterprise setup as well as the principal owner's wishes when it comes to the level of direct control of future generations. Legal ownership is a direct form of ownership and control that offers the owner all the rights and privileges associated with owning the property or entity. Beneficial ownership offers the beneficial owner the privileges associated with the property or entity, rather than the actual ownership and decision-making rights of it. Choosing the optimal legal and ownership structure requires careful reflection by the founder(s), who must consider what their overall intentions are while considering their specific context.

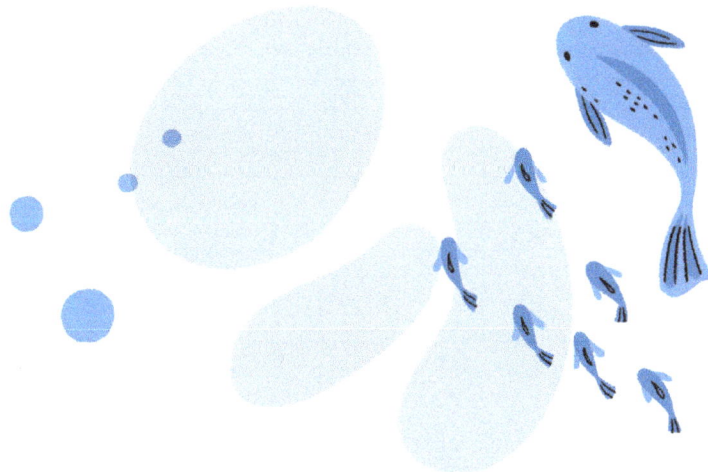

ACTIVITIES

The following activities will help you and your family clarify questions related to the resources you need for your family office.

Family Office Navigator questions:

- What types of resources do we need (talent, partnerships, infrastructure, back office)?
- How do we finance the family office?
- What is the right legal and ownership model?

ACTIVITY 1:
FAMILY OFFICE TALENT

Now that we have explored the different dimensions of your family office resources, we invite you to reflect on each of these dimensions in your family group. Evidently, each of these aspects are highly technical matters and we appreciate that it will take more time as well as outside guidance and support to navigate them. Nonetheless, we invite you to have a structured conversation as a family before seeking outside support, to ensure that you can lead the conversation rather than be led.

Some guiding questions that you need to consider are:

- What roles need to be filled in the family office?
- What are key responsibilities of each role?
- What skills and competencies should families look for when hiring non-family members for the family office?
- How should compensation for family office executives be structured?
- Which roles can or should family members play in the family office?
- What are the benefits and drawbacks of having family members in certain roles?

Having a good advisor for this step can be decisive given the importance of hiring the right people into your family office. We would not recommend families venture into this phase without the necessary external advice.

Step 1:
Roles and responsibilities

As a family, reflect on the different roles and responsibilities that you consider essential for your family office, keeping in mind your family office's overall strategic direction, as well as the services you consider important and whether you think they should be handled in-house or not. You can simply start by populating a list, possibly supplemented by a short description of what you would expect each of these roles / positions to do in the family office.

Step 2:
Family members' involvement

Consider which of these roles could be filled by the family, depending on the family's wish to be involved as well as the family members' skills and capabilities. You can also discuss the advantages and disadvantages of having family members involved in the operations of the family office (as opposed to being involved only in the overarching governance and control bodies).

Step 3:
Defining target profiles, compensation principles
and next steps for the recruitment of key employees

Start defining the job profiles and the types of compensation schemes (including incentive mechanisms) you consider adequate and consider how to find the right person. At this stage, we recommend that you primarily focus on a high-level discussion rather than going deeper.

ACTIVITY 2

As a family, go through the following table and put in some ballpark numbers with respect to each of the cost items of the family office. This is meant to get the discussion going and raise awareness of the key cost drivers to ensure that there are no surprises later in the process. The numbers will vary considerably from one family office to the next and therefore the process of completing this activity is more important than the actual numbers that you put in. As with everything, it will likely cost more than you think in the end.

Step 1:
Complete the table as a family

Item	Setup cost	Annual cost	Comments / assumptions
Personnel (salaries, bonuses, incentives, social insurance)			
Headhunter fees to search for key functions			
Office (rent, services, furnishing, deposits, refurbishing)			
IT infrastructure (hardware, software, maintenance, connectivity, servers, security)			
Legal, tax and audit			
Travel and representation expenses			
Administration fees			
Insurances			
Other			

Step 2:
Financing

Once you have filled in the table, have a discussion as a family about how you plan to finance the setup and running costs of the family office. There are many different approaches for financing – again, the intention here is to start the conversation rather than to come up with a final answer. In any case, the ultimate choice you make is contingent on a multitude of complex factors that you will most likely be able to address only with the right expert partner on the ground.

ACTIVITY 3:
OPEN DISCUSSION AROUND SEVERAL RESOURCING QUESTIONS
(FOR THOSE THAT DO NOT YET HAVE A FAMILY OFFICE)

We recommend you have an initial, open discussion as a family about the key questions related to setting up the family office, the resources involved and any legal and ownership matters.

GOVERNANCE AND MONITORING

Setting the scene

Good governance and oversight play a crucial role in maintaining family cohesion and ensuring the long-term continuation of the family enterprise ecosystem. Effective governance is essential for family offices, given their responsibility to safeguard family wealth and reputation. By carefully designing decision-making procedures - from business and investment decisions to philanthropic and family-specific decisions - the family and the family office can achieve alignment across the family enterprise ecosystem and ensure that the family's overarching goals are translated into specific actions on all levels within the system.

In this section, we will explore the different aspects of governance within the family enterprise ecosystem - including family, ownership, business and investment governance - and discuss how these aspects should be aligned to ensure maximum effectiveness and efficiency in the system. We will dive deeper into the specifics of family office governance to ensure that the family is always in the driver's seat. It is vital that the family have the right tools in hand to monitor the performance of the family office.

Family office governance should focus on overseeing activities to ensure proper authorization, effective control and alignment with risk, compliance, and cost parameters. Additionally, it should ensure that the mandate of the office align with the family's vision, even as the vision evolves with changing family dynamics.

WHAT DO WE MEAN BY GOVERNANCE?

Governance is the system of rules, processes, and structures that help you direct and control an organization. While this might sound complicated, there are many examples and best practices of good family office governance which will help you set up and run a successful operation as part of your family enterprise ecosystem.

At the basic level, good governance requires the harmonious combination of a number of key elements, as highlighted in the pyramid below.

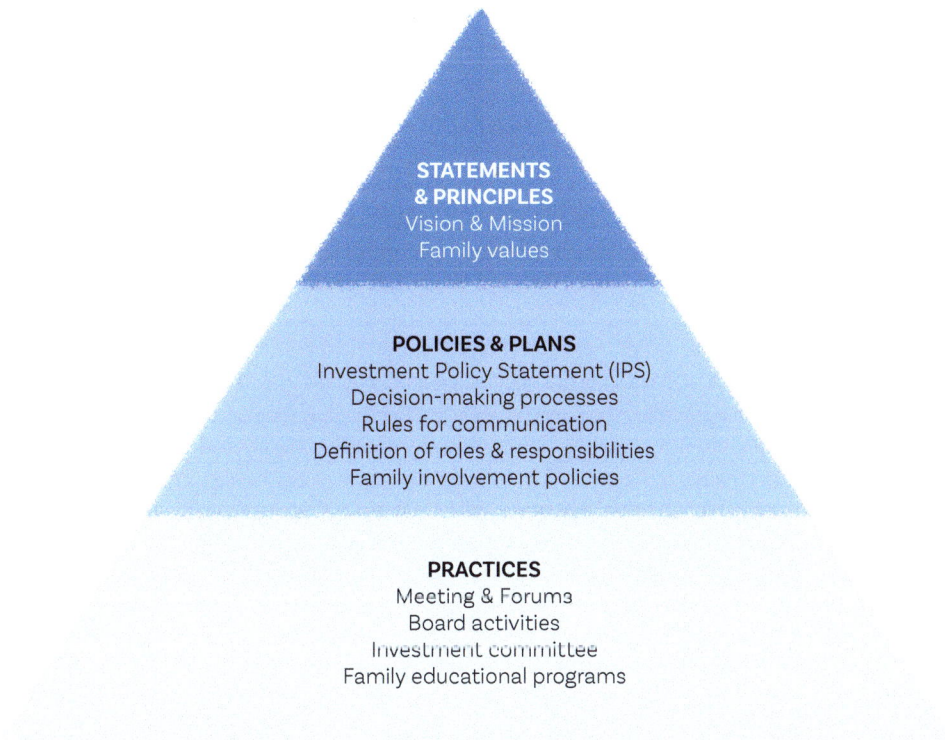

STATEMENTS & PRINCIPLES
Vision & Mission
Family values

POLICIES & PLANS
Investment Policy Statement (IPS)
Decision-making processes
Rules for communication
Definition of roles & responsibilities
Family involvement policies

PRACTICES
Meeting & Forums
Board activities
Investment committee
Family educational programs

Inspired by the Family Governance Pyramid by Patricia Angus, 2005

Family office governance as part of the family enterprise ecosystem

The ultimate governance decisions for your family office are contingent on several factors related to your family enterprise ecosystem, as outlined in previous chapters. Is there an overarching purpose that connects what we do in business, investments and philanthropy? How do the family office activities fit into the wider range of activities of the family, the ownership group and the business? What are the strategic connections between the different activities of the family within the wider system? Is the family office linked to other parts of the system or are they consciously kept separate? Do we want to strategically leverage the family office for other activities, such as the operating business? What role does the family council play in our ecosystem and the family office? What role should the family office play in educating and onboarding the next generation?

These are just some of many questions you and your family ought to ask when it comes to embedding the family office within the wider ecosystem. It is worth considering how you could make your family office activities cohesive and aligned with existing governance structures, protocols and values within your family, ownership group, and business.

This holistic view is particularly useful for the purposes of the *Family Office Navigator* as it allows families to unlock synergies, ensure long-term continuity, while also providing reassurance to the family. If you already have a family office in place, this is an opportunity to reassess your current governance principles to ensure it is fit for purpose and appropriate for your family, especially the current or next generation.

The graphic below builds on the well-established "three circle" model, illustrating the family, business, and ownership groups and the main governance mechanisms that you might consider leveraging for your family office activities.

Remember, all family enterprise ecosystems are unique, and you might not necessarily need to put in place all these governance mechanisms. You also wouldn't necessarily leverage all of them at once. Instead, the "three-circle" model intends to provide an overview of different possible connections with your wider governance model.

Three circle model including governance mechanisms

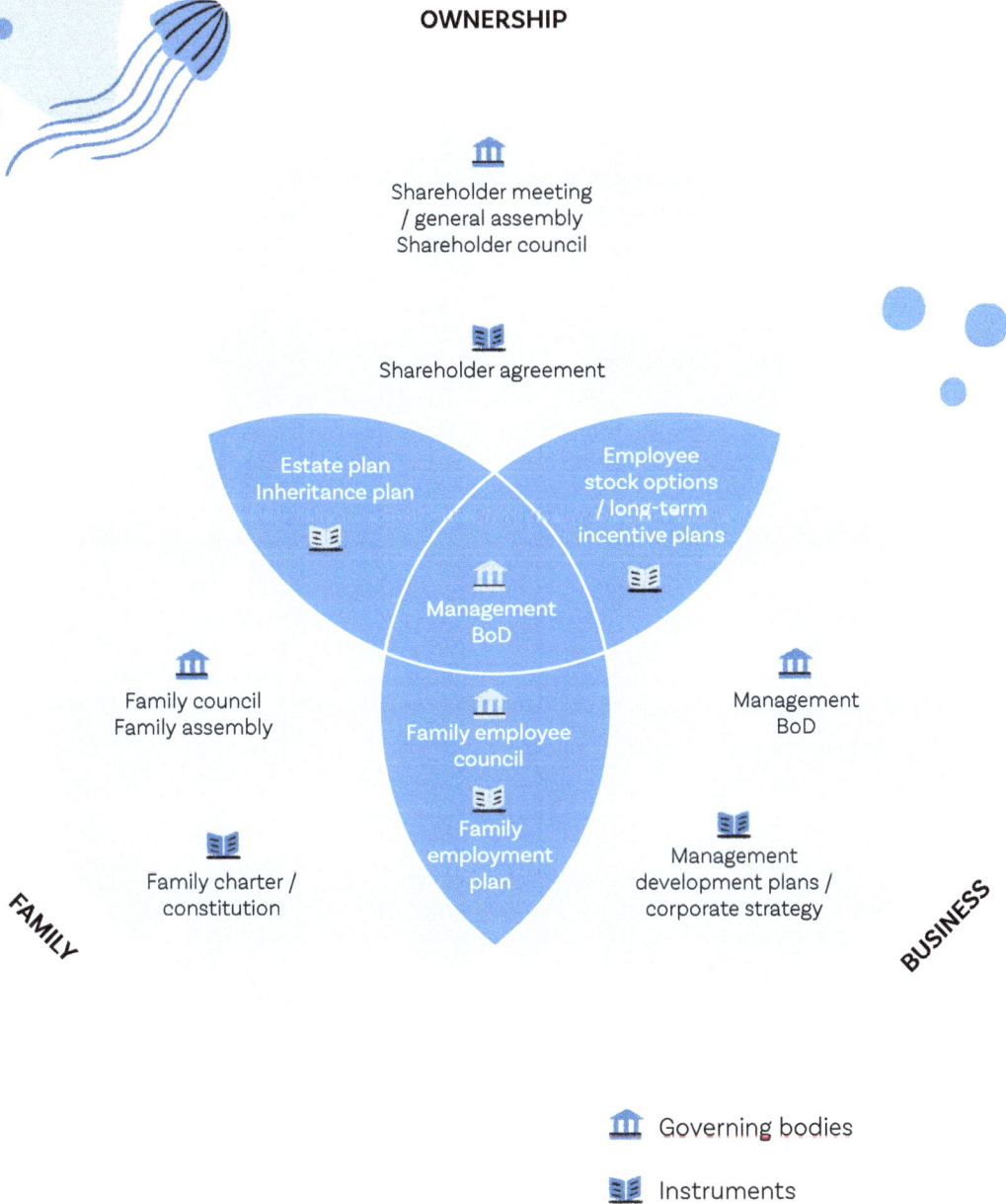

OWNERSHIP

Shareholder meeting
/ general assembly
Shareholder council

Shareholder agreement

Estate plan
Inheritance plan

Employee
stock options
/ long-term
incentive plans

Management
BoD

Family council
Family assembly

Family employee
council

Management
BoD

Family
employment
plan

Family charter /
constitution

Management
development plans /
corporate strategy

FAMILY

BUSINESS

Governing bodies

Instruments

Framework: Tagiuri and Davis, 1982
Source: Generation to Generation, Gersick / Davis / McCollom / Lansberg

Family governance

Here is a high-level overview of some of the most essential family governance mechanisms and how they relate to family offices.

Good family governance is essential to ensure family unity and effective and timely decision-making. While this is straightforward in the founder stage of a business, it becomes more complex as families grow in complexity. Decision-making authority becomes more dispersed across siblings, cousins or family branches and requires effective governance bodies to ensure that the system can function well and that sources of potential family conflict are, as much as possible, dealt with in a structured manner.

While all the different entities within the family enterprise ecosystem (businesses, investment vehicles, philanthropic organizations and so on) have their own governance mechanisms (such as boards of directors, statutes, shareholder agreements, strategy documents), family governance allows the family to manage itself and provides structured guidance to the various entities and governing bodies that reside within the ecosystem. Such an orchestrated approach is paramount for the healthy functioning of larger family enterprise systems and typically gains in strategic importance as the system grows. While initially a lot of attention is put on the core operating entity, families put a stronger emphasis on family matters as the system matures and a larger, more diversified group of activities emerge. Hence, family governance can become the main strategic entity within the ecosystem.

Family assembly

As family enterprises are passed down to subsequent generations, authority tends to become more decentralized. To navigate this, families often create a family assembly – an annual gathering of eligible adult members. The assembly serves a dual role: it's an information nexus, illuminating business and familial dynamics, as well as an educational epicenter, fostering financial and operational acumen. Beyond fact-sharing, assemblies interweave serious family matters with social endeavors, strengthening familial ties and ensuring cohesion. The family office can play an important role in organizing these family gatherings. This can be of great help to the part-time family volunteers who typically run the different family governance activities and end up organizing these types of events - especially in the context of larger families.

Family council

In a family enterprise, especially a sizable one, the family council operates as a pivotal working committee, effectively acting on behalf of the broader family assembly. The council convenes multiple times a year, playing a key role in shaping and fine-tuning vital components such as the family's values, mission, vision, and overarching policies. Serving as the bridge between the family and the board or owners, the family council ensures robust governance, overseeing the financial aspects of the family's dealings. Moreover, it is entrusted with the crucial task of conflict resolution, mediating any disputes that arise within the family. Through its actions, the council aids in maintaining the harmony, vision, and longevity of the family enterprise, all while keeping the broader family assembly informed and involved.

The family office can function as the logistical backbone for the family council. It assists in organizing council meetings, maintaining records and even publishing family newsletters. Crucially, while the family council requires funding for its operations, such as event organization, the family office manages these funds once sanctioned by the family assembly. Beyond administrative support, the family office is an invaluable collaborator. It communicates family interests and concerns, proposes strategies to uphold family values and provides key financial insights. For instance, it can uniquely correlate family enterprise results with individual family members' financial positions. Furthermore, the family office can ensure the impartial selection of next-generation members for roles within the enterprise, promoting transparency in hiring. If a family lacks a family council, the family office can either help establish one or even take on some of its responsibilities, including crafting the family's vision and mission statements. In its role of communicator, planner, educator and mediator, the family office acts as the essential hub of the family enterprise.

The existing family and ownership governance bodies are highly influential in overseeing and shaping the role of the family office. While there are, of course, formal governance mechanisms to consider for the family office, including boards and investment committees, we find that larger families, in particular, establish committees or working groups – either within the family council or separately – to ensure that all family office activities are aligned with the wider family's needs and interests and that all family members, especially those who are not so much involved in the daily operations of the business or the family office, are kept informed.

In the "Charting your Course" chapter, we introduced the view of the evolutionary nature of the family enterprise ecosystem and that, with increasing complexity, the scope and mandate of the family office will vary. It is time to bring back the overview we shared in that chapter and dive into a little more detail.

	Typical characteristics	**Some structural considerations for a family office**
Founder / controlling owner stage	• Small family (often 1st or 2nd gen) • Central position of controlling owner • Leadership & governance dictated by founder / controlling owner • Little complexity in the family enterprise system • Wealth is highly concentrated in the business • Liquid wealth derived from profitable operations or liquidity event leading to sudden wealth	• Most likely a pure investment office (at least in the beginning) • Potentially a few additional custom services, depending on the particular needs and wants of the family (for example, concierge services)
Evolving / maturing family business stage	• Increasing family size (often 3rd generation onwards) • Ownership distributed across branches of the family • Family may be in operational roles or may lead only in governance and ownership roles • Increased complexity of the system, particularly regarding governance • Increased risk of conflicts (between siblings, cousins, branches,…) • Business has grown, likely diversified, sometimes reaching conglomerate stage • A large proportion of the family's assets are bound in the legacy business until a liquidity event happens • Investable wealth derived from profits from legacy operations, sale of a company, or fast-growing new ventures	• Investment office with mandate to slowly start building a portfolio of assets • Supporting the family with specific needs (e.g., education of NxG, governance, etc.) • Some additional custom services
Large / dynastic family enterprise stage	• Large family (50+ family members across multiple branches, no more distinct generations) • Large complexity of the family enterprise system • Diversified portfolio of assets • Oftentimes, the family is no longer in a leading operational role in the legacy business (if they still have one)	• Managing the family's portfolio of assets • Organizing various governance forums for the family • Supporting the family with talent development • Supporting the family with unity-building and relationship-building • Providing concierge services

The nature of a family office will look fundamentally different across the different stages of evolution and its governance will change accordingly. Governance in the earlier stages is a lot less complex than in later stages. Typically, in the beginning, decision-making and oversight is dominated by the principal wealth owner – the patriarch or matriarch. While this is an easy and efficient governance approach, it poses major risks in the context of succession as it requires a fundamental governance overhaul, just as in a family-controlled enterprise. In later stages of evolution, with ownership and decision-making spread out across multiple branches and generations, governance evolves and becomes more structured and complex.

Decision-making

How will investment decisions be made? How formal or informal should the decision-making process be? Which governing bodies take which decisions? No matter what type of setup you and your family select, decision-making is a critical part of your family office. When designing your decision-making processes, there are important factors such as family dynamics, family size, family structure, as well as any existing ways of taking family decisions that you need to consider.

It is important to clearly spell out the process and rules for decision-making with regard to your family office activities, otherwise you might end up in a conflict situation that could have easily been avoided. We suggest that you and your family first reflect on the full range of decision-making options that you could apply, select the most appropriate option for your family, and only then start the process of actually taking decisions.

Decision-making can be an incredibly time-consuming and frustrating process even if you have an explicit, structured approach: other family dynamics can kick in and bypass the formal governance you have created. In this case, the family culture takes over and makes any formal governance structures obsolete. A very typical challenge arises when one board member (the founder or parent, for example) has more influence than others and, as a result, his or her opinion implicitly carries more weight. This can be particularly frustrating for the next generation or for outside advisors or board members who have been hired to help professionalize operations. It is therefore important that all family members understand and, as much as possible, follow the governance the family has agreed on.

As in business, different decisions might require different decision-making approaches. Here are three common approaches:

Unilateral decision-making	Voting by majority	Consensus-based decision-making
• This approach is a quick and efficient mechanism that is useful for minor or uncontroversial matters, as well as decisions that need to be made in a very short time. • We typically find this type of decision-making in the early phase of a family office before formal governance structures are in place. • Unilateral decision making is common in enterprising families, oftentimes because there is one dominant family member.	• This approach might be required by the by-laws for a certain type of decision. It involves all board members and leads to a definite outcome based on whether a majority is reached or not. • Board voting with majority can be a useful mechanism in case there are many interconnected governance activities within the family enterprise ecosystem that require transparency and alignment. • Voting is often considered as a fallback option in case consensus cannot be reached.	• Consensus-based decision making may be required by the by-laws for very important decisions (e.g., discontinuing the family office) and is a mechanism that typically involves a lot of discussion, thus resulting in a shared understanding and buy-in. • Consensus-based decision-making can be a sign of a very healthy and functioning family, ownership group, or business board. We have observed that high-performing corporate boards decide based on consensus quite naturally and only in rare instances resort to voting by majority. • However, in case of different views and perspectives, which you will inevitably have in a family and even more so if you involve multiple stakeholders from the family enterprise system, this can be a very time-consuming process. Any attempt to reach consensus might trigger other forms of conflict (depending on family dynamics), which is why it might not be the most appropriate form of decision-making for every family and every decision.

It is of critical importance that you clearly spell out who, or which governing body, will take what type of decisions and based on what type of decision-making mechanism. Aligning this with your overall governance will help you establish a more effective and efficient family office, as part of your wider family enterprise ecosystem.

Effective family office boards

Depending on the legal structure of the family office, you might be obliged to have a board of directors. Boards are vital in many family office journeys for decision-making, oversight, as well as to empower and involve family members and other partners. Depending on the nature and mandate of the family office, the board and the investment committee could be one body. However, it is advisable to separate these functions, especially in family offices with a wider range of services and activities. While the family office board takes a more holistic view of the family office, the investment committee should focus specifically on investment activities. Depending on the size and setup of the family office, the investment committee could be a sub-committee of the board. Some families also opt for an advisory board which is less formal, with the main purpose of gaining access to independent, external expertise.

To ensure your board is fit for purpose, it is important that you ask yourself several questions related to board composition, structure and policies.

Board composition

- Do you include just the immediate family or also the extended family?
Can in-laws have a seat on the board? What happens in case of a divorce? Do you award your children seats on the board?
What are the minimum and maximum age limits for board membership?
- Do you want non-family and independent professionals to join the board? If so, what would be their role and level of participation?
If not, how would you source subject area expertise to support a family-only board?
- What are the responsibilities of each board member?
How will board members be sanctioned or removed if they fail to meet these responsibilities?
- What type of knowledge and expertise do you wish to gain access to by adding independent board members?
- How does your board relate to your mission and strategic priorities?
What challenges would the current composition of your board tackle?
- What will be the link between the investment committee and the board of directors?

Board structure

- How many board members do you wish to include?
How many family members can join?
- How often does the board meet?
- Do you wish to establish committees (e.g., investment performance, finance committee) within the board or not?

Board policies

- How is board membership shared among siblings and family branches? What are the criteria for selecting family and non-family board members? Are there any pre-requisites in terms of skills, capabilities and expertise in order for family members to be considered for a board role?
- What policies do you need to put in place to bring clarity to the board, now and in the future?
- What are the term limits and rotations?
- What tools can the board use to streamline the planning process?
- How can the board and staff communicate effectively?
- What is the conflict resolution policy?

Why family office governance fails

Good governance is paramount in any organization. Yet there are many reasons why the governance of family offices may not work in the most effective and efficient way. Governance failures in family offices can arise due to a complex interplay of family dynamics, a lack of clarity and resistance to external input. The main reasons for failure are:

- **Disconnect with wider governance:** The family office's governance doesn't align with the broader family enterprise ecosystem, leading to inconsistent decision-making and goals.
- **Unclear family role:** The responsibilities and influence of family members within the family office are not defined, leading to potential overlaps or gaps in decision-making.
- **Resistance to oversight:** Wealth owners may desire autonomy over their assets, shunning effective governance mechanisms and external professional guidance.
- **Ambiguous decision-making:** Decision-making processes within the family office lack clarity, resulting in inefficiencies and conflicts.
- **Lack of family guidance:** Without clear directives on the family office's mandate, goals, and ambitions, the office lacks direction and purpose.
- **Narrow governance focus:** While the governance bodies might be proficient in investment oversight, it may neglect the broader tenets of good governance, compromising holistic management.
- **Poor onboarding of the next generation:** Failure to educate and integrate the next generation can lead to discontinuities and misalignment in future leadership.
- **Limited transparency:** Some active family members in the office may not provide sufficient transparency or independent evaluation, causing mistrust among other family members.

- **Inadequate understanding within the governance body.**
  The governing body might:
  - Lack comprehension of investment activities, risks, and repercussions.
  - Be ill-equipped to gauge the quality of outcomes.
  - Fail to assess if the current path aligns with overarching goals.

Dealing with conflict in the family

Even the most efficient governance systems can fail to prevent conflict. The reality is that there is no perfectly conflict-free environment. It is no different in the context of family offices. Here are some common sources of family office conflict to watch out for:

1. **Investments:** Where do we invest? How much? What if our investments are not working out well?
2. **Control:** How do we control our investment decisions / performance over time?
3. **Funding the family office vs. benefitting from services:**
   Are we all contributing equally? Are we all benefitting equally? If not, what do we do?
4. **Role:** Can a specific family member have an important role in the business and family office, or might this trigger conflicts of interest or unfair treatment vis-à-vis other family members?
5. **Rivalry:** Do we have branch representation or merit-based representation in our family office?
6. **Multigenerational tensions:** Is the senior generation holding on to decision-making and control or can the next generation take responsibility?

Having independent experts on the board or in the investment committee will not only bring knowledge and ideas to the table, but also help the family to have constructive discussions even when the performance is not meeting expectations. They can shield the family from feeling tempted to blame specific members of the committee.

Investment governance

While traditional family business systems will focus on establishing solid governance mechanisms for the family, the ownership group, and the business, the evolution of a family office requires the creation of world-class investment governance as a fourth governance pillar, which acts independently of, but in concert with, the other governance mechanisms in the family enterprise ecosystem.

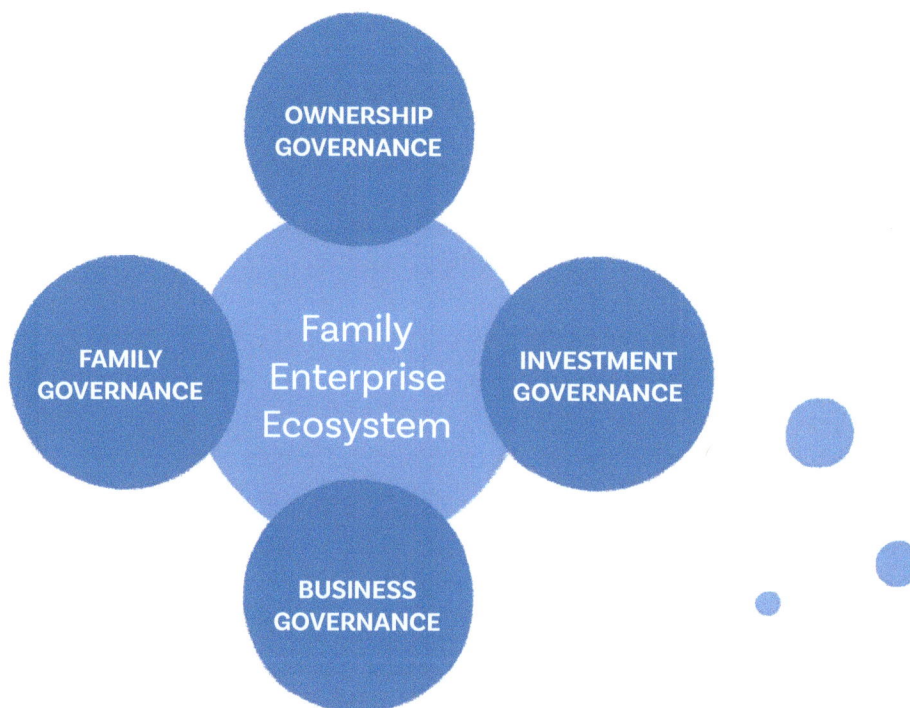

OWNERSHIP GOVERNANCE

FAMILY GOVERNANCE

Family Enterprise Ecosystem

INVESTMENT GOVERNANCE

BUSINESS GOVERNANCE

The main difference between investment governance for a family office and the family's other governance mechanisms is that there is a need for technical knowledge and a basic understanding of the investment world. Families need to be mindful that not everybody in the family has the necessary skills or interest in financial matters. No matter what the level of engagement of the family will be, establishing a system of investment governance will ensure that the family has the necessary control and oversight of the family office.

Fundamentally, investment governance is very similar to corporate governance. It is important that family members establish a world-class investment committee, mixing family talents with external talents to ensure independent expert insights and a healthy balance of power when it comes to critical decisions.

Corporate Governance	Investment Governance
Shareholders	**Family Owners**
Board of Directors	**Investment Committee**
CEO & Executive Board	**Chief Investment Office & Family Office Executives**
Corporate Functions	**Internal Team**
Outsourcing Partners	**Outsourcing Partners**

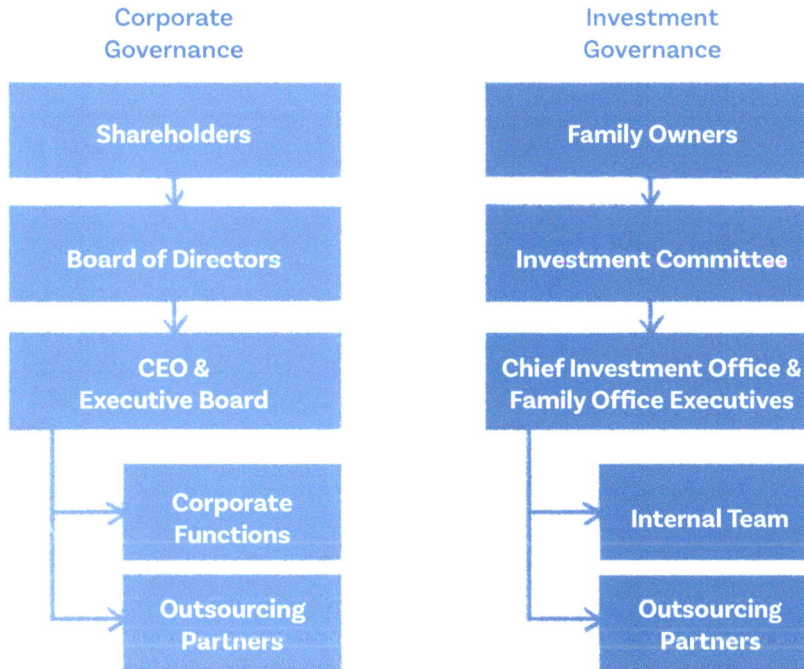

Effective investment governance brings together some key governance principles and mechanisms, including the investment committee, guidelines, policies, reporting, controlling, and monitoring. Let's explore these in more detail.

Investment committee

The role and mandate of an investment committee in a family office is vital to the successful stewardship of family wealth. While the specifics might vary depending on the unique needs and structures of individual family offices, the committee's core responsibilities encompass setting and aligning investment strategies with the family's objectives, rigorously monitoring performance, conducting due diligence on external managers, and formulating key governance policies, notably the Investment Policy Statement (IPS). The committee ensures that all investments align with the IPS and provides a lens through which the family office's performance is assessed, both in terms of returns and on a risk-adjusted basis. It must objectively assess and challenge investment proposals from the investment team as well as the family to ensure full alignment with the overarching, long-term investment strategy.

Investment committees typically include the family office president / CEO, the CIO, selected family members, as well as selected external specialists.

The intensity of the committee work depends on a variety of factors but, similarly to a board of directors, the frequency of meetings can vary from monthly to quarterly, with additional meetings in between, where needed. The investment committee plays a key role in reporting the investment performance to the family or the family office's board of directors.

Investment policy

Investment policies are unique to each family, depending on your specific goals, needs, and risk profile. The investment policy clarifies the goals and objectives of the family as to how their wealth should (or should not) be invested and what their expectations are. This, in turn, serves as guidance to the family office team as well as external service providers to ensure that whatever investment proposals they make are aligned with these guidelines. The investment policy document also serves as a record for the specific decisions that the family has taken regarding investment principles and the investment approach.

An Investment Policy Statement (IPS) is typically drafted in an iterative process, merging family-specific needs and concerns with general best practices (concentration limitations, rebalancing rules, etc.). As economies, markets, and the family's needs and appetite for risk change over time, the IPS needs to be revisited frequently and either confirmed or modified.

The following table provides an overview of the main elements of an IPS.

Purpose & scope	What are the objectives and scope of the investment policy? What asset classes should be covered?
Definitions	Roles and responsibilities of various governing bodies, documents, and key third parties, as well as clarification of terminologies within the policy framework.
General guidelines	This is the core of the document and provides the guiding framework for the investment strategy: • Investment philosophy • Investment objectives (quantitative and qualitative) • Short- and long-term liquidity needs / constraints • Investment structure • Risk tolerance • Return expectations • Time horizon • Reference currency • Distribution policy • Liquidity policy • Use of leverage • Taxation considerations • Legal and other constraints

Portfolio investment policies	This section defines and describes the long-term strategy: • Asset allocation policy • Direct investment policy (filter criteria / exclusion, portfolio management, deal wall, etc.) • Diversification policy (concentration limits) • Acceptable deviations from the allocation • Rebalancing • Additional restrictions
Risk management, monitoring and reporting	This section specifies risk parameters and clarifies how reporting and monitoring should be managed: • Definition of observed risk factors • Reporting scope and frequency • Investment controlling mandate

Here is an exemplary process for creating an investment policy statement.

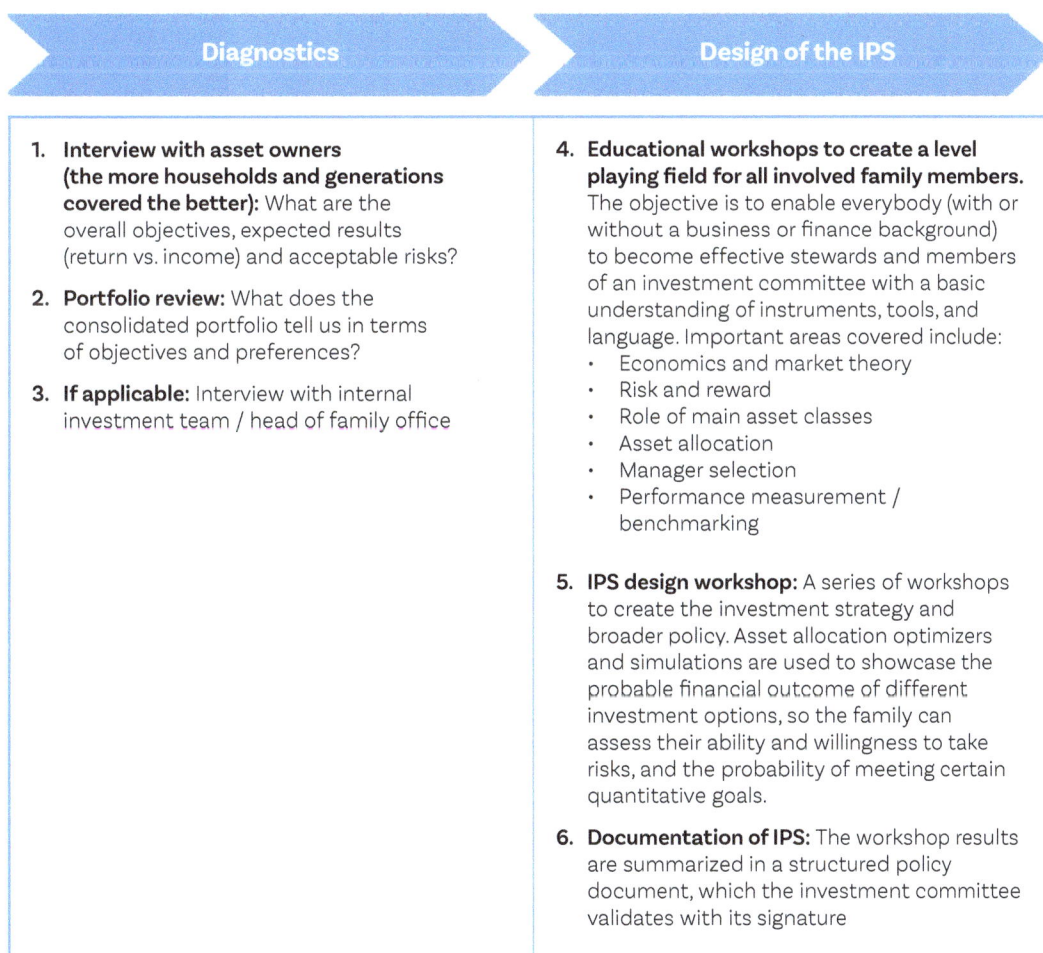

Diagnostics	Design of the IPS
1. **Interview with asset owners (the more households and generations covered the better):** What are the overall objectives, expected results (return vs. income) and acceptable risks? 2. **Portfolio review:** What does the consolidated portfolio tell us in terms of objectives and preferences? 3. **If applicable:** Interview with internal investment team / head of family office	4. **Educational workshops to create a level playing field for all involved family members.** The objective is to enable everybody (with or without a business or finance background) to become effective stewards and members of an investment committee with a basic understanding of instruments, tools, and language. Important areas covered include: • Economics and market theory • Risk and reward • Role of main asset classes • Asset allocation • Manager selection • Performance measurement / benchmarking 5. **IPS design workshop:** A series of workshops to create the investment strategy and broader policy. Asset allocation optimizers and simulations are used to showcase the probable financial outcome of different investment options, so the family can assess their ability and willingness to take risks, and the probability of meeting certain quantitative goals. 6. **Documentation of IPS:** The workshop results are summarized in a structured policy document, which the investment committee validates with its signature

Reporting, controlling and monitoring

No business operates without a monitoring and controlling function. Investment controlling is a specialized function which helps the family keep track of what's going on in the family office and regularly benchmarks the family office against peer groups in the market. Ideally, this function is run independently from the family office to ensure a "four eyes" principle, which is comparable to an external audit in a business. Besides assessing the quality of the results, it is indispensable to track whether the overall portfolio remains aligned with the IPS. Reporting forms a central part of controlling.

Here are some key points to bear in mind with respect to investment reporting:

- Assets and liabilities are typically scattered across asset managers / custodians and consolidated reporting is therefore an important prerequisite for risk management and sound investment decision-making.
- The valuation of assets, performance computation, benchmarking, and reporting independent from asset managers significantly reduces conflicts of interests and the risk of errors and fraud.
- Designing your custom report allows you access to information you need to effectively supervise investments, identify issues and manage risks.

Investment controlling distills information and highlights where attention is needed:

- **Benchmarking:** How does the risk-adjusted return compare to markets and peer groups?
  - Consolidated portfolio?
  - Individual managers / strategies?
- **Manager supervision:** Are our investment managers operating within the agreed strategies?
- **Compliance:** Is our portfolio operated within the set investment guidelines (risks, liquidity, concentration, etc.)?
- **Fee monitoring:** Are investment-related costs within the agreed terms? Is there potential for any reduction?
- **Objective tracking:** Is our portfolio on track to deliver the set objectives (return, income)?

Own your analytics

Working with families from around the globe, we see that the world of investments has become increasingly fragmented and complex, and that it is difficult to keep track of all the activities that take place within a portfolio. Working with a diverse range of service providers such as banks, brokers and asset managers adds to this challenge. It is important that families have a system in place that allows them to maintain control of their investments and their family office.

Monitoring the family office

Regular monitoring of a family office by the ownership group is paramount to ensuring the office's strategies and operations align with the family's objectives and values. Continuous oversight provides clarity on the family office's performance, risk management, and alignment with the family's evolving goals. Key aspects to consider include the office's adherence to the investment policy statement (IPS), the effectiveness of its governance structures and the clarity and frequency of its reporting. It is also vital to watch for potential conflicts of interest, especially when the office is making investment decisions or selecting external advisors. Ensuring transparent communication, maintaining an updated understanding of the family's long-term vision and actively addressing any operational or ethical concerns promptly are critical for the successful synergy between the ownership group and the family office.

Here are a few things to keep in mind when it comes to monitoring your family office:

Does the family office meet our needs?

- Do we know what we need from the family office?
- Is the family office helping us achieve our multigenerational goals?
- Is the service we receive of the required quality?

Do we have the right oversight of the family office?

- Do we have the right governance in place?
- Do we have the right people to make decisions?
- Does the family office serve us or are we dependent on the family office?

Do we have the right infrastructure?

- Do we have our risks under control (financial, security)?
- Do we have the necessary transparency?
- Do we have the right talent?

Are performance and costs in line with our expectations?

- Do we have transparency on our costs?
- Are our operating costs commensurate to the services? How do they compare to other SFOs?
- How does our performance compare to the market?
- Are the risks taken in line with our IPS and the risk appetite of the family?

ACTIVITIES

The following two activities will help you and your family answer critical questions as you decide on the most appropriate governance and monitoring structures for your family office. Keep in mind that the family office you decide to set up should reflect your family enterprise ecosystem and your family manifesto, it should match the purpose you've chosen for your family office and cater to your specific needs through its range of services. As such, it is advisable to go through these activities with your answers to the previous activities at hand.

Family Office Navigator questions:

- How do we govern the family office?
- How will we connect the family office governance with other mechanisms in the system?
- How do we measure our family office performance? What are our metrics of success?
- Are these aligned with our family manifesto and purpose?

ACTIVITY 1:
ALIGNING ON KEY GOVERNANCE PARAMETERS

Step 1:
Map out the status quo

As a family, map out the current governance mechanisms and systems that you have in place within your family enterprise ecosystem. It might be of help at this stage to refer back to the overview of your entire ecosystem that you mapped out in the "Charting Your Course" chapter.

Governance mechanism	Currently in place	Comments (needs to be created, needs to be updated, ...)
Family governance		
Family assembly	☐ yes ☐ no	
Family council	☐ yes ☐ no	
Family constitution	☐ yes ☐ no	
Ownership governance		
Shareholder assembly	☐ yes ☐ no	
Shareholder council	☐ yes ☐ no	
Shareholder agreement	☐ yes ☐ no	

Step 2:
Identify possibly links with your family office activities

Once you have mapped out the family and ownership governance mechanisms that exist in your family enterprise ecosystem, you can start thinking about possible links and connections with your family office activities. How much integration between the family office with other activities do you wish to have? Are there any "gaps" in your current governance that you think need to be filled to advance your cause?

Step 3:
Map out your initial thoughts on decision-making

Now, take some time to think about how you would like to take decisions and which governance bodies you wish to put in place for your family office:

- Which decisions would we like to take as a family, and which governing body should take them (family council, family office board, Investment committee, etc.)?
- How will we take decisions as a family (on projects, financial matters, strategic matters…)?
- Which decisions do we delegate to other governance bodies within our family enterprise ecosystem?

ACTIVITY 2:
MAP OUT YOUR INVESTMENT POLICY STATEMENT (IPS)

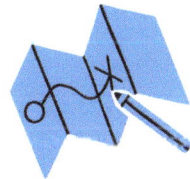

Building on the process outlined earlier in this chapter, it's time for you and your family to start mapping out your investment policy statement. It is advisable to engage a professional facilitator with experience in family workshops and, more specifically, the design of investment policy statements to help you with this step. This will improve the management, impact and outcome of your reflections and ensure the creation of a best-in-class IPS.

This IPS canvas will help you structure your reflections.

PURPOSE AND SCOPE

What are the overall objectives and scope of the investment policy? What asset classes should be covered? Which parts of the family enterprise are out of scope, if any?

DEFINITIONS

Roles and responsibilities of various governing bodies, documents, and key third parties, as well as clarification of terminologies within the policy framework.

INVESTMENT GUIDELINES

This is the core of the document and provides the guiding framework for the investment strategy:

- Investment philosophy
- Investment objectives (qualitative and qualitative)
- Short-and long-term liquidity needs / constraints
- Investment structure
- Risk tolerance
- Return expectations
- Time horizon
- Reference currency
- Distribution policy
- Liquidity policy
- Use of leverage
- Taxation considerations
- Legal and other constraints

PORTFOLIO INVESTMENT POLICIES

This section essentially defines and describes the long-term investment strategy:

- Asset allocation policy
- Direct investment policy (filter criteria / exclusion, portfolio management, deal wall, etc.)
- Diversification policy (concentration limits)
- Acceptable deviations to the allocation
- Rebalancing
- Additional restrictions

RISK MANAGEMENT, MONITORING AND REPORTING

This section specifies risk parameters and clarifies how reporting and monitoring should take place:

- Definition of observed risk factors
- Reporting scope and frequency
- Investment controlling mandate

CONCLUSION

Congratulations! You have now completed the "Family Office Strategy House" and have successfully navigated through the entire *Family Office Navigator*.

Take a moment to reflect on the impressive work you've accomplished:

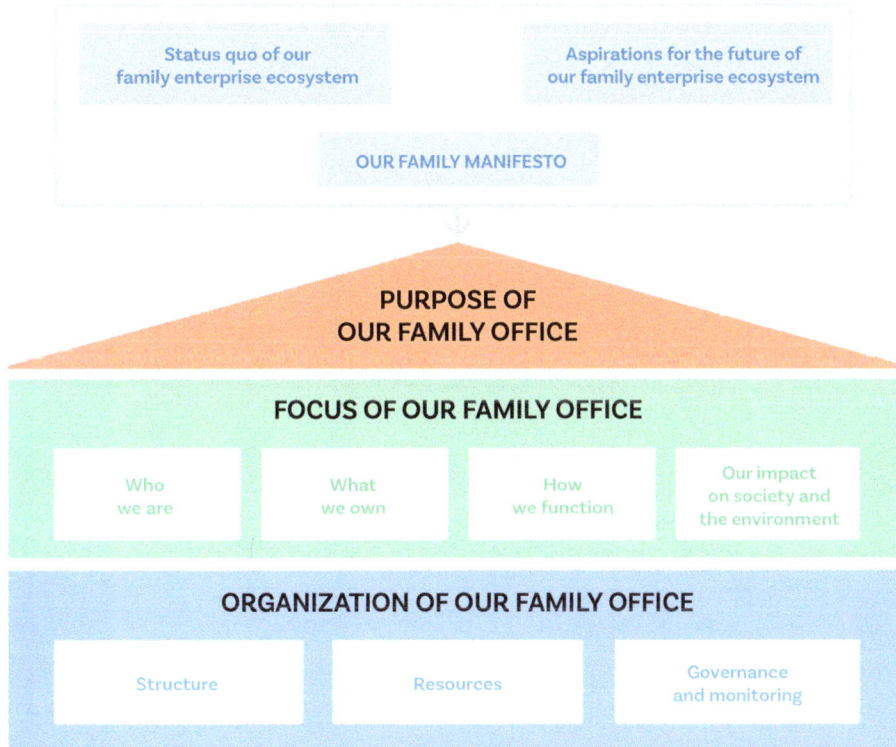

- You've mapped out both your existing and future family enterprise ecosystems and formulated your family manifesto.
- You've addressed questions regarding the purpose, focus, and organization of your family office.

With all the building blocks in place, you're ready to embark on your family office journey. Before moving forward, we invite you on one last exploration, emphasizing the significance of continuous learning and reflection as vital components of your family office journey. It's crucial to establish regular checkpoints where you and your family review the work done over the past months or years. These moments will help assess whether you remain aligned with your overarching goals or if there's a need to adjust your course of action.

CHAPTER 6

LEARNING

Charting a thriving family office journey through intentional learning and reflection.

ORIGINAL PLAN

"For the things we have to learn before we can do them, we learn by doing them."

Aristotle

DEVELOPING A LEARNING STRATEGY

A common trait of high-performing family offices is that they develop a learning strategy and culture that enables them to adapt and improve on a continual basis. As part of the learning and evaluation process, the following questions merit reflection at regular intervals:

Is your family office running effectively and efficiently? Are you still focusing on the right services and activities or is it time to change course? Are your asset allocation choices well aligned with your overarching family purpose? Have there been major changes in your family enterprise ecosystem that justify a rethinking of your overall direction and strategy? Are the other members of your family still committed? Do you have the right partners to implement your strategy? Could you change something to have greater impact? How do you learn from your experiences so that you can, over time, improve your family office?

This final section of the *Navigator* will explore and describe how to embrace the notion of learning during your journey so that you can continue to build and maintain an effective and healthy family office.

Learning plays a crucial role in life, in general, and in the context of family enterprises and family offices, in particular. Why? Because your family enterprise ecosystem is constantly changing and, as such, the family office also needs to evolve and adapt to these changing parameters. You should have regular quality checks and learning loops to assess where you stand, where you would like to go, and what kind of adjustments are necessary as a result. If you do not embed a learning and reflection culture into the core of your activities, you risk losing out on effectiveness in your family office.

There are many ways to learn, and we all have our preferred learning styles. There are several differentiations to consider when it comes to learning:

1. Learning can happen in the moment, or it can happen reflectively. Both ways of learning can be a valuable source of insights and knowledge in your family office journey.
2. Learning can happen by acquiring new knowledge in a conceptual manner or it can happen "on the job." In the context of family offices, we need to be mindful in applying one or both of these learning strategies optimally.
3. Learning can happen alone or together with others. As much as we learn from our own mistakes and successes, we also learn from others who have embarked on this journey before us. However, for various reasons (e.g., privacy and safety of the family, cultural or religious norms) many families decide to be rather discreet about their family office activities, which can make sharing with and learning from others tricky. Nonetheless, we see in our work the value in families learning together in a safe, confidential and solicitation-free environment.

Learning by doing – a caveat

"Learning by doing" is a useful approach for launching new ventures since it allows us to go out and explore different options. A hands-on approach also offers an engaging, pragmatic and creative way to learn. And while this approach is also necessary in the context of family offices, we recommend caution, because certain mistakes – especially when it comes to investment decisions – can be very costly. Therefore, families need to carefully assess the willingness to "invest" in this type of learning by potentially making mistakes. In our work with families, we frequently hear them tell us that, especially in the beginning of the family office, they made some costly mistakes because they did not have a proper investment strategy in place yet, leading them to suboptimal investment decisions that they regretted afterwards.

Which activities are truly value-adding to your family and which ones could be discontinued, outsourced, or improved? Are the people we onboarded in the family office the right type of talents? Is decision-making happening the way we envision it? Are family members excited about the family office and is communication happening well? These are questions you should be asking yourself at regular intervals. Especially in the first years after launching the family office, where a lot of fine-tuning might be necessary. You can never get all factors right from the beginning but, through careful learning and reflection, it is possible to understand why certain aspects of your family office journey might have been suboptimal and what improvements you could make.

Think renewal

Each organization has its own life cycle – from creation to termination. This is no different for family offices. Across this cycle, families must manage or at least oversee the operational challenges of establishing and running a family office, such as start-up and running costs, management and administrative costs, and taxes. Beyond this, there are other challenges to be met and overcome, for example, dispersed multigenerational interests when it comes to asset allocation choices or diverging goals and priorities over time. Being prepared to renew your family office while instilling a spirit of continuous learning and improvement will help to ensure your activities remain relevant and effective. Our experience shows that motivations often remain consistent over generations but priorities can change.

Linking learning to the Navigator

Learning can trigger a pivot within any of the different dimensions of the *Family Office Navigator*, whether it's mapping out your current and future family enterprise ecosystem, your family manifesto, or the purpose, focus and the organizational setup of your family office. We recommend that you regard learning as an integral and continuous part of your family office journey rather than as a separate activity that only happens when something goes wrong or at a specific time of year. Learning should be embedded as an ongoing component of your family office activities and reflections.

Learning at the start of the journey

For families that are just about to start their family office activities, it is less important to think about changing your course of action immediately, because you're just getting started. However, it will be helpful to integrate learning as a key element from the very beginning so that it becomes part of your culture and you can learn and improve as you go. You will want to think about how, today and in the future, you will want to systematically embrace the notion of learning to ensure that you are on the right track or, if not, how you want to adjust the course.

In the early stages of your family office journey, it is important that you remain flexible and show a willingness to learn and adjust. That way you can gradually professionalize your activities, learn from your mistakes quickly and ensure that you achieve maximum effectiveness as quickly as possible. Exchanging with and learning from more advanced family offices is a great way to start. Don't shy away from speaking with other families in your network and openly asking them about their learnings and what advice they might have for you.

Learning for ongoing development and course correction

For more established family offices, the exercise of completing the *Navigator* and assessing whether you wish to make any changes to one or more dimensions of the *Navigator* is already an act of reflection and learning.

Over time, you may want to consider incorporating a more formal and regular way of learning, which could include a regular review of the core dimensions of the *Family Office Navigator*. You might want to specify a mechanism for, and the frequency of, a more formal review process and additional learning activities.

We encourage you to work with outside experts to offer you a neutral outside-in perspective on what you are doing, to help identify potential blind spots and areas for improvement.

Some key questions you might want to ask yourself:

· How can we create a culture of learning inside the family as well
  as inside our family office?
· How can we ensure that those who are involved in our family office –
  family members, non-family professionals and partners – fully embrace
  the mindset of learning? How can we learn together?
· How can we improve learning from others while, at the same time,
  act as a role model for others and share our experience?
· How can we connect learning with the evaluation of our family office?

Insights from the field

We conducted dozens of interviews with families that have an established family office, asking them what their biggest learnings and recommendations are. Here is a summary of some of their key insights:

Theme	Key learning insights from families
Purpose	It is essential that you and your family develop a clear family purpose before you do anything with your family office. Otherwise you run the risk of navigating without a compass and we know how that might end if the weather turns bad.
	Leverage your wealth and privileged position to do something that you are passionate about and that makes a difference in the world. This is a unique opportunity and also a responsibility that we all share.
Governance	It is important that everybody in the family has a solid and shared understanding of what you wish to accomplish and where you wish to go.
	A major risk for families is that they do not spend enough time to create the necessary alignment within the family before engaging in specific investment activities. It is of disproportionate importance to take along the less financially savvy family members.
	In our case it was beneficial to keep the family and business activities and governance separated. However, it required an extra portion of coordination and alignment.
	Make sure to keep the entire family close to the family office. This is particularly important as the next generation is emerging. Next generation education is key.
	Devote as much time as possible to keep the family together and close to one another.
	You need to first establish all the necessary governance mechanisms before you embark on this journey. It will become more difficult to do so at a later moment in time, especially in moments of crisis when you would need good governance.
	When a family member runs the family office operationally, you need to ensure that there is non-family supervision from the board.
	The collaboration and coordination between the family office and the family council is a key success factor for the family enterprise ecosystem. It must not be underestimated in terms of efforts needed to make this work smoothly.
	The family office ideally becomes the central trusted advisor of the family members. It therefore owns deep knowledge of individual family members and the family as a whole.
	The family should, as much as possible, be involved in the family office. If not hands-on then at least in the governance and oversight. But it is fatal to assume that you can simply delegate everything and close your eyes, hoping for the best outcome.

Investment	Take your time to devise a proper investment strategy first and don't jump at the first opportunity that presents itself. As soon as you establish yourself in the field of investments you will be confronted with more opportunities to invest than you can realistically can (or should) consider investing in.
	Start simple and take your time in the beginning. The biggest (and most costly) mistakes typically happen in the beginning because the family is eager to get going and a nervousness develops, blurring decision-making.
	Make sure you diversify your assets.
Learning Mindset	Be humble. There are many families that are much more advanced in this that you can learn from. Go into this with a beginners' mindset.
	Don't assume that just because you were successful with an operating business and now achieved some financial success through a liquidity event that you know everything when it comes to managing that money. Arrogance or ignorance in this phase is the best recipe to lose it all.
	The biggest mistake we made was to embark on this journey thinking we know it all. But in reality, we didn't know anything and lost a lot of money. Money that was created over generations.
Partners & Suppliers	Hire professionals early on in the process and don't try to do everything by yourself.
	One of the most important things that you will need help with is to navigate the landscape of financial service providers.
	Trusting relationships with partners are essential in this journey.
	Beware the private wealth managers. If it is your own money you need to learn how to manage it yourself, even if (ultimately) you end up delegating it to others. If you do not have the tools to manage it yourself then you will also not be able to supervise others that well. You can delegate some things but not everything. As owner you need to have the ultimate oversight.
	If someone gives you advice you need to make sure that no one else is paying them to give you that advice.
	Build a strong network of strategic and (as much as possible) independent advisors, who can help you navigate the space without being conflicted.
Strategy & Organization	It is essential to think about everything in a more holistic way and to consider establishing an enterprise strategy, thinking across the different dimensions of Total Family Wealth.
	As in any business one needs to clearly define the skills and competencies that one has and that one needs for every role that exists within the family office. Professional talent management is key to success.
	There's always more demand for FO services than you think. Therefore, define a clear service offering of your FO and find the right trade-off between individualism and scalability.
	You cannot assume that the principles that work for your operating business will also work for your family office. These are two fundamentally different types of entities.

Building a learning culture and organization

Families and their family offices engage in learning for a variety of reasons. First, learning helps them perform at the highest possible level. Moreover, families leverage learning as a vehicle to foster dialogue and exchange amongst family members, as well as with their family office team and partners.

With the purpose of learning in mind, a useful concept that family offices can apply is the learning organization model. The idea of a learning organization emerged in the field of business management as a way to reinvent the classic top-down corporate structure to create a system of continual growth and learning, collaboration and intelligent risk-taking. The goal of a learning organization is to emphasize personal and professional growth through knowledge transfer. A culture that encourages learning and curiosity, in turn, enables an organization to continuously transform itself and remain relevant in a competitive business environment.

As you reflect on the learning culture that would best fit with your family office endeavor, remember that learning is also a great way to shape and refine your strategy. Instead of trying to think of the most effective and efficient way to do things, you can engage with the ecosystem around you to come up with better ideas, test new concepts for the family office and then shape and refine them. By establishing a learning culture and learning organization, you can also ensure that it's acceptable for everyone that you go back and constructively review some of your ongoing activities to shape the path forward. Ultimately, learning is a critical way of thinking and working when it comes to assessing the outcomes of projects you have completed. Learning is an essential aspect of every successful family enterprise and should be leveraged strategically in order to learn across generations.

Learning together with your family and your partners

It is important that learning becomes an integral part of your family's values and activities. Being curious, inquisitive and open to new knowledge and experience is incredibly relevant when a family wants to ensure that their family office works towards their family's overarching purpose and achieves the desired results. You can leverage many of the aspects of the *Navigator* as a vehicle for collective learning, across generations. It is a fun and engaging way for families to learn together, especially when it comes to the less technical aspects of the *Navigator*, such as mapping out your family enterprise ecosystem, designing your family manifesto and defining the family office purpose.

Setting up a culture for learning is often handled through existing governance bodies such as the family council and can also be supported by family office executives. The senior generation in the family, as well as family members who are in leading governance roles of the family office, need to signal a willingness as well as a commitment to learning and then onboard the wider family. This is critical for the next generation to grow into such a way of thinking and working. The ability of each generation to learn and renew your organization will be key to achieving sustainable multi-generational unity and success.

ACTIVITIES

In the following table we will share a few initial questions you can ask yourself when it comes to evaluating your family office activities. While this is primarily geared towards established family offices, we still advise families that aspire to launch a family office to review this list carefully as it might help you shape your journey moving forward.

***Family Office Navigator* questions:**

- What are our mechanisms for learning and for adjusting the course, if necessary?

Step 1:
Review the different dimensions of the *Family Office Navigator* and assess each of them by rating them from 1-5

Dimension in the *Navigator*	Question	Strongly disagree 1	2	3	4	Strongly agree 5

YOUR FAMILY ENTERPRISE ECOSYSTEM

		1	2	3	4	5
Status quo of the family enterprise system	The family has full clarity and understanding of our current family enterprise ecosystem.	●	●	●	●	●
Aspirations for the future	As a family, we have defined our aspirations and outlined what our ideal family enterprise ecosystem will look like in the future.	●	●	●	●	●
Family manifesto	We have a created a family manifesto (including the family's vision/purpose, reasons for being together as a family, family values) that offers the necessary guidance for our family.	●	●	●	●	●

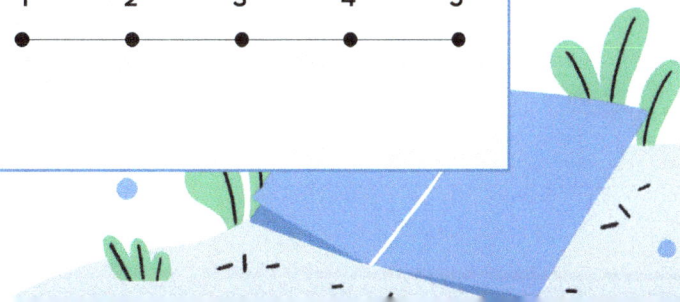

PURPOSE

		1	2	3	4	5
Statement of purpose	Our purpose for the family office is clearly defined and provides the necessary direction to the work of the family office.	●	●	●	●	●
Coherence of purpose	Our family office purpose is aligned with our family manifesto.	●	●	●	●	●

FOCUS

		1	2	3	4	5
Definition of focus	We have clearly defined the focus (scope of activities and services) of our family office.	●	●	●	●	●
Pertinence of services	The range of family office services reflects the needs, expectations and complexities that exist within our family enterprise ecosystem (who we are, what we own, how we function, our role in society and the environment).	●	●	●	●	●

ORGANIZATION

		1	2	3	4	5
STRUCTURE	The current structure of the family office is well designed and suited to serve its purpose.	●	●	●	●	●
RESOURCES	We have all the necessary resources (talent, partnerships, infrastructure, IT, back office, etc.) in place to efficiently operate our family office.	●	●	●	●	●
Family employment policy	We have clearly defined who from the family is involved in our family office activities and what the nature of their involvement is.	●	●	●	●	●

		1	2	3	4	5
Family performance	Family members deliver on the work that they have committed to.					
Family involvement	Family members are actively engaged in our activities (attend meetings, read newsletters, participate in visits, etc.).					
GOVERNANCE	Our family office governance is effective and provides the necessary guidance and oversight for the family office.					
Coherence	We have clarity on how the family office's governance is embedded into the overall / wider governance of the family enterprise ecosystem.					
MONITORING	We have effective systems of reporting, controlling and monitoring in place.					
KPIs	We have established well-defined measures of success / Key Performance Indicators (KPIs).					
Performance	Overall, our family office operates successfully and is working towards our family manifesto while achieving its targets.					

LEARNING

		1	2	3	4	5
Evaluation process	We regularly review the performance and the priorities of our family office to ensure that they are aligned with our family manifesto.					
Learning mindset	Learning helps us to remain on the cutting edge in our family office activities.					

Open questions

What is one aspect of your family office that you would like to preserve?

What is one aspect of your family office that you would like to change?

Do the various dimensions from your *Navigator* align or are there inconsistencies?

Step 2:
Review and compare the results with your family members
Identify similarities and differences in your responses

It is important to note that these evaluations are subjective measures indicating the feeling and thoughts of respondents. Nonetheless, alignment amongst family members on a specific item should provide a reliable indication as to whether things are going well or could be improved. Below are general guidelines for interpreting the results of the questionnaire:

1. If you have diverging points of views on certain aspects, we advise you to engage in an open and constructive discussion to better understand each other's perspectives.
2. If you collectively gave a certain dimension a high score (4 or 5), this is an indication that it is an area of strength for your family office. You may wish to make note of it for future reference as it can be useful to build your long-term strategy around the family office's agreed-upon assets and strengths.
3. If you collectively gave a certain dimension a low score (1 or 2), this signals an area of weakness for your family office that should be discussed and, ideally, addressed with an improvement strategy.

Clearly, this is only the starting point of a more thorough and in-depth learning process. This last activity is closely linked to the different dimensions of the *Family Office Navigator*, and we recommend that you and your family carefully review each of those steps and have an in-depth conversation about what has worked well, what could be improved and, most importantly, what changes you feel are necessary to make moving forward.

BEYOND THE NAVIGATOR

Embarking on the next phase by transforming the *Navigator* insights into actionable steps for a vibrant family office future.

«"...throw off the bowlines, sail away from safe harbor, catch the trade winds in your sails. Explore, dream, discover.»

Mark Twain

Journey's end, progress's beginning

You have now completed the *Family Office Navigator*. We hope that you have found the book and toolkit to be accessible, helpful and inspiring in designing or redesigning your family office.

In our fast-paced world, where family enterprise ecosystems become more complex and wealth and asset management become ever more intricate, our ultimate aim through the *Navigator* has been to help you and your family become more effective in setting up or repurposing your family office. We hope this method has served as both a steady anchor and a reliable compass for your family office journey.

It is our aspiration that upon completion of this book you will have formulated clear answers on the most important questions relating to your family office endeavor:

- What does our family enterprise ecosystem look like today and what will it ideally look like in the future? What do we wish to achieve together as a family?
- What is our family manifesto? Why are we better off together than alone? What are our family purpose and values?
- What is the purpose of our family office?
- What will be the core activities and services of our family office?
- How will we organize our family office to ensure that it can fulfill its purpose?

You have now carefully mapped out your strategic plan by defining the purpose, focus and organizational design of your future family office. These decisions and clarifications will form the foundation and fuel for the next steps in your family office undertaking. There is only so much preparation, reflection and finetuning you can do. At some point you will have to put your model and ideas to the test in the real world. You and your family may not always get it right, and you will most likely make changes to the strategic choices you made as part of the *Family Office Navigator* activities, but it is now time to make your move. This is the exciting part.

The *Navigator* was designed to serve as a reliable guide for families at any stage of their family office journey – not just as a handbook for establishing a family office but also a guide to challenging the status quo of an existing family office and making adjustments where needed. For this reason, we recommend that you revisit the *Family Office Navigator* in a structured way with your family at regular intervals in the future, depending on your circumstances. This could be a regular review of the core elements of the *Navigator* to make sure you are on track and aligned with your initial plan and purpose. It could be a comprehensive exercise every few years to work through each step of the *Navigator* from scratch as a 360° health check of your activities. You could also take a deep dive into one aspect of the *Navigator*, such as governance, family involvement or focus, if you feel that it is necessary or if something has changed that requires a new approach.

A call to action

For now, the best way to take your *Navigator* insights and bring them to life is through the creation of an action plan for you and your core team. This will provide the structure and deliverables that will keep you on track as you implement your reflections and learning.

There are many ways to build an action plan, and many existing, proven models. Like each aspect of the *Navigator*, there is no right or wrong way to plan ahead. The best is to agree on a path forward and design a plan, together with your family, in a way that works for you. Nevertheless, in doing so, it might be useful to cover the following questions.

- As a family, what actions do you need to perform?
- What are your priorities, and how do you decide on them?
- What are your timelines and milestones?
- Who will take charge of which action items?
- How will you deal with reporting on progress within your different governance bodies?

It could be that you read through the *Family Office Navigator* alone without including your wider family. That is perfectly fine. That being said, we recommend that, before you take any concrete actions, you take everyone from the family along with you on your journey. It is of vital importance, as we highlighted throughout the book, that this be an inclusive process. Take the necessary time to share your thoughts and what you have learned or invite the other family members to read the *Family Office Navigator*, too.

Also, please check the *Navigator* book website for updates and useful tools, videos and other materials: **www.imd.org/fon**.

Further reading & learning

We covered a lot of ground in this book, but we are sure you will agree that we could have gone much deeper into every single dimension of family offices that we examined. Nonetheless, we purposefully chose not to make the *Navigator* too technical in nature because our aim was to create an inclusive tool – accessible for all family members – to learn about and develop your own family office.

If you wish to go deeper into certain aspects we covered, below is a list of publications we recommend:

- Canessa, Boris, Jens Escher, Alexander Koeberle-Schmid, Peter Preller, Christoph Weber. **The Family Office: A Practical Guide to Strategically and Operationally Managing Family Wealth**. Springer, 2018.
- Rosplock, Kirby. **The Complete Family Office Handbook: A Guide for Affluent Families and the Advisors who Serve Them**. Wiley, 2020.
- Somers, Mark. **Family Office Fundamentals – Human Capital Matters: The Principal's Guide to Creating, Staffing and Future-Proofing your Family Office**. Independent Publishing Network, 2023.
- Woodson, William, Edward Marshall. **The Family Office: A Comprehensive Guide for Advisers, Practitioners, and Students**. Columbia Business School Publishing, 2021.

> You might also enjoy reading the *Family Philanthropy Navigator*, an inspirational guide for philanthropic families on their giving journey. The *Family Philanthropy Navigator* was designed to help families be more strategic and more impactful in their giving in order to thoughtfully make a difference in the world. You can find more information about this publication on: **www.imd.org/fpn**.

Last but not least, if you wish to deepen and consolidate what you have learned in the *Family Office Navigator* in the form of an educational program, please reach out to us. Our flagship program "Leading your Family Office" is designed for families to embark on a learning journey together: **www.imd.org/lfo**.
We will also happily explore tailored learning journeys with you.

Bon voyage!

It has been a pleasure and privilege to accompany you on this trip through the *Family Office Navigator*. Please do not hesitate to contact us anytime you have questions or wish to discuss your family office endeavor. We wish you and your family all the best for your next steps. May your family office journey be rewarding, enjoyable and impactful for you and your family.

Also in the same series:

Family Philanthropy Navigator

The Inspirational Guide for Philanthropic Families on Their Giving Journey

by Peter Vogel, Etienne Eichenberger
and Małgorzata Smulowitz (-Kurak)

ABOUT THE AUTHORS

Peter Vogel

Peter is Professor of Family Business & Entrepreneurship and the Director of the Global Family Business Center at IMD Business School. Peter works as a trusted advisor to enterprising families as well as their boards and top teams, focusing on transformations, governance, ownership- and leadership succession, business model questions, wealth management and high performing teams. He has authored numerous books and articles, and he is a sought-after speaker. He is founder of Delta Venture Partners and Associate Partner of CFEG.

Mario Marconi

Mario was a senior advisor and partner at the Cambridge Family Enterprise Group, and an Executive-in-Residence at IMD Business School. A former UBS private bank executive, he was an expert on family office design and management, with extensive experience advising families globally on financial strategies for private wealth and business needs. Mario recognized the broader purpose of family wealth, and enjoyed working with families to make the world a better place.

IMD
Real learning
Real impact

IMD and the Global Family Business Center

IMD is an independent academic institution with campuses in Lausanne and Singapore. For more than 75 years, IMD has been a pioneering force in developing leaders who transform organizations and contribute to society. IMD's executive education and degree programs are consistently ranked among the world's best by the Financial Times, Bloomberg, Forbes and others. This consistency at the forefront of its industry is grounded in IMD's unique approach to creating "Real Learning. Real Impact". Led by an expert and diverse faculty, IMD strives to be the trusted learning partner of choice for ambitious individuals and organizations worldwide. Challenging what is and inspiring what could be.

IMD has been a pioneer in the field of family enterprises and was the birthplace of family business education back in 1988. For 35 years we have been working with families, owners, board members and executives of family businesses, family offices and family foundations, helping them ensure family unity, business and investment success as well as a positive impact on society and the environment, for generations to come.

CAMBRIDGE
FAMILY ENTERPRISE GROUP®

Cambridge Family Enterprise Group

Cambridge Family Enterprise Group (CFEG) is a global advisory, education, and research organization that serves family enterprises with growth aspirations, enabling them to flourish across generations. Based in Cambridge, Massachusetts (U.S.), CFEG has advised and educated thousands of families from more than 70 countries since its founding in 1989 by Professor John Davis. Its pioneering thought leadership, methodologies, and strategies are used by family enterprises worldwide to achieve lasting success.

As trusted advisors, educators, and researchers, CFEG offers a wide range of services to families, family offices, and family businesses. CFEG is a go-to trusted resource and partner for the world's enterprising families to navigate changing times, develop future-ready strategies, grow long-term value, architect succession transitions, develop key talent, address family dynamics, design ownership, governance, and organizations, and achieve multigenerational success. CFEG takes a collaborative, multidisciplinary, and solutions-oriented approach to co-create with families the practical and sustainable pathways for their continued growth and success. With CFEG, families climb higher and generate an even better future.

FBN

In partnership with the Family Business Network (FBN)

FBN is the world's leading organization of business families. "By family businesses" and "for family businesses," FBN is a safe, shared-learning space for enterprising families to flourish across generations, through the exchange of excellent, innovative and impactful practices.

Founded in 1989, it is headquartered in Lausanne, Switzerland. A vibrant community, it brings together over 4,500 business families – 20,000 individual members including 8,000 NxG members – in 34 Chapters covering 70 countries.

Annually FBN organizes thousands of online and offline activities and programs internationally, regionally and locally. It brings together communities tailored to different generations, roles and topics: NxG, NowGen, Polaris, Entrepreneurship, Family Office and Large Families.

Milton Keynes UK
Ingram Content Group UK Ltd.
UKHW052012060824
446607UK00008B/46

9 782940 485376